Reprint

The Black Ox
A Study in the History of a Folk-Tale

Archer Taylor

Fathom Publishing Company

Introduction and images copyright © 2017 Ann Taylor Schwing. Reproduction or translation of any part of this work beyond that permitted by Section 107 or 108 of the 1976 United States Copyright Act without permission in writing from the copyright owner is unlawful. Requests for permission or further information should be addressed to the publisher.

ISBN: 978-1-888215-72-4
Library of Congress Control Number: 2017959292

Orginally printed in FF Communications No. 70, Helsinki, 1927.
Suomalainen Tiedeakatemia, Academia Scientiarum Fennica.

Fathom Publishing Company
PO Box 200448
Anchorage, AK 99520-0448
www.fathompublishing.com
www.archertaylor.com

Archer Taylor

Archer Taylor (center) on an Atlantic cattle boat during a summer trip to Europe during his Swarthmore years.

Archer Taylor (left) with a friend and his sisters.

Introduction to
English Riddles from Oral Tradition Reprint

Archer Taylor was born August 1, 1890 and died September 30, 1973. He was called Archer because the family had difficulty agreeing on a name, and his uncle began calling him Sagittarius, symbolized in Greek mythology by the archer—half-man, half-horse in the ninth astrological sign.

Taylor wrote many books and a vast number of articles, some extended studies of the subject at hand and others short notes or queries. He grew up in a world in which academic-minded students learned Latin and Greek in grammar school, and he learned. In the years that followed, he continued to learn. Ultimately he read and spoke thirteen languages, with varying degrees of proficiency to be sure. In high school and early college years at Swarthmore, he worked on a cattle boat to Europe at the start of the summer. Once there, he traveled to the various countries in Europe learning the languages and meeting the people before returning to port to sign on a boat for the trip home. These experiences left him with a love of language and languages (and a life-long dislike for marmalade, pumpernickel and salt pork, the only foods for the crew on the voyage once the fresh things had been eaten). These experiences ended with World War I when he was caught in Europe at the start of the war and had to make his way home. His family sought news of his location and condition in the flyer shown on the next page.

After finishing Swarthmore in three years, Taylor taught and studied, earning his M.A. at the University of Pennsylvania and his PhD at Harvard and publishing his dissertation on the Wolfdietrich epics in 1915. He taught at Washington University in St. Louis starting in 1915, moving to the University of Chicago for the years 1925 into 1939. He ended his teaching career at the University of California, Berkeley, where he served from 1939 to 1958 and was chairman of the Department of German from

Mr. ARCHER TAYLOR, born August 1st, 1890, West Chester, Pennsylvania, U. S. of America, Father, American born Citizen, Lowndes Taylor, West Chester, Pennsylvania.

Instructor and Assistant Professor for two years at "State College" Pennsylvania.

Specialty, German Language and literature.

He went to Europe in June 1914, to persue special studies toward his Ph. D degree.

He was last heard from by postal mailed Wilhemlshohe, (Bz. Cassel) Germany.

In that postal he announced his intention to go at once to Gottingen.

He gave his address as "Archer Taylor, Dresden, Poste Restante. Germany.

But he has acknowledged no mail so addressed to him.

He has visited Germany several times on summer tours, and is somewhat familiar with the people and their language.

He speaks also a little French.

He is a graduate of Swarthmore College, a Quaker Institution, and also of the University of Pennsylvania.

He was studying at Harvard University for his Doctor's Degree, and went to Germany sssisted by Swarthmore College.

He had sufficient Credits for ordinary purposes and usual expenses in times of peace.

Please assist him in any way possible, also give any information of him to the German Police, and inform the local American Representatives, (Consul &c.)

Also kindly send information pegarding him to his uncle, Ervine D. York, Flushing, New York.

Or to his father,
Lowndes Taylor, West Chester, Pennsylvania,
U. S. of America.

1940 to 1945. Taylor published *The Proverb* in 1931, followed by *Index to the Proverb* in 1934. His Bibliography of Riddles was published in 1939, and a number of other riddle books followed. Archer Taylor and Bartlett Jere Whiting published *A Dictionary of American Proverbs and Proverbial Phrases*, 1820-1880 (Cambridge, Massachusetts: Harvard University Press (1958). Although much of his writing concerned folklore, he also wrote *A History of Bibliographies of Bibliographies* in 1955 and *General Subject-Indexes Since 1548* was published in 1966. Other books and an extraordinary number of articles flowed from his ongoing research, and these were the years before computers and word processing. My sister and I remember alphabetizing yellow 2x3 slips he prepared, one for each proverb.

Taylor married Alice Jones in 1915, and she bore him three children, Margaret, Richard and Cynthia. Alice sadly died early in 1930, and he married Hasseltine Byrd in 1932 and fathered with two more children, Mary Constance and Ann.

A collateral benefit of his teaching position at the University of California was that Taylor could send his professional mail through the University. He carried on a prodigious correspondence with individuals and journals of similar interests around the world. When these individuals came to California, they often stopped to visit and to discuss their scholarship. A fascinating example of one series of letters is collected at http://www.rtp.pt/acores/comunidades/archer-taylor-to-a-young-literary-folklorist-an-exchange-of-letters---george-monteiro_40888. More is collected at http://sh.diva-portal.org/smash/get/diva2:560414/FULLTEXT02.pdf and https://nirc.nanzan-u.ac.jp/nfile/1054. Former students became close friends, illustrated by the friendship between Wayland Hand and Taylor that lasted the rest of Taylor's life.

His large library is now with the University of Georgia in Athens, excepting his ballad collection with the University of California, Berkeley. In addition to collecting books himself, Taylor watched for books and collections that he knew were sought by universities around the world. He might buy and send the desired books or notify the university so it could buy them. He was honored after World War II for his extended efforts to rebuild the university library in Dresden.

Wolfgang Meider published one of the reprints of *The Proverb* and posted a Biographical Sketch at http://locustvalley.com/business/Families%20of%20Distinction/Taylor.html.

In 1960 Archer Taylor was rightfully and deservedly honored by a most impressive "Festschrift" which his two friends Wayland D. Hand and Gustave O. Arlt edited with the befitting title *Humaniora, Essays in Literature, Folklore, Bibliography, Honoring Archer Taylor on His Seventieth Birthday* (Locust Valley/New York 1960). The subtitle summarizes Taylor's three major areas of expertise and such internationally renowned contributors as Bartlett Jere Whiting, L. L. Hammerich, Dag Strömbeck, Stith Thompson, Walter Anderson, Taylor Starck, Kurt Ranke, Lutz Röhrich, Matti Kuusi, Georgios A. Megas, Robert Wildhaber, Francis Lee Utley, Anna Brigitta Rooth, Will-Erich Peuckert, Wolfram Eberhard, Julian Krzyzanowski, etc. acknowledge Taylor's worldwide influence.

"Archer Taylor The Paremiologist," a detailed biography, was printed in De Proverio, Volumne 2, No. 1, 1996 and is available online at https://deproverbio.com/archer-taylor-the-paremiologist/.

Archer Taylor lived and died with friends around the world. He never passed up opportunities to explain and teach—the difference between anecdote and antidote, for example, when a teenage daughter got it wrong. He generously shared his knowledge and curiosity with all.

Ann Taylor Schwing
November 2017

FF COMMUNICATIONS N:o 70

THE BLACK OX

A STUDY IN THE HISTORY OF A FOLK-TALE

BY

ARCHER TAYLOR

HELSINKI, 1927
SUOMALAINEN TIEDEAKATEMIA
ACADEMIA SCIENTIARUM FENNICA

Haminan Lehti Osakeyhtiön
kirjapainossa, Haminassa 1927

The Black Ox:

A Study in the History of a Folk-tale.

In Finland a strictly systematic method has long been employed in the study of popular traditions. An exemplification in English of the method will show the English reader what advantages it may have and will give greater opportunity for criticism and improvement. Such an exemplification should deal with a tale which is not unduly complicated in narrative structure — lest the argument become too involved to follow easily — and which is brief enough to permit the presentation of all the versions (at least in abstract) so that the reader may verify any particular assertion or deduction or may even do the whole study over according to his own ideas. For this purpose I have selected the Finnish tale of the "Black Ox." A preliminary study of this tale is already available;[1] and, moreover, since there are no literary versions of importance, the field is narrowed to purely traditional or popular material.

Of the "Black Ox" more than a hundred versions have been recorded in Finland. This number is sufficiently large to enable us to determine with some degree of accuracy both the details of the normal form and the various centers of distribution. Since no very considerable differences are noticeable in these versions, it is possible to construct any prototypic form with more than the usual confidence, though

---

[1] Kaarle Krohn, "Musta härkä eli Lapissa käynti", *Kotiseutu*, 1916, No. 4.

a certain amount of doubt must, of course, always be present in any such reconstruction.

Such a tale as the "Black Ox", and probably every tale in circulation among the folk, is at the same time a definite entity and and an abstraction. It is an entity in the particular form in which it happens to be recorded at any moment; it is an abstraction in the sense that no two versions ever exactly agree and that consequently the tale lives only in endless mutations. The life-history of the "Black Ox" may with some justice be said to be a contradiction in terms, for we have not stopped to define of which version of the "Black Ox" we shall write the history. The establishment of the normal form is consequently the process of defining just what we mean by the "tale of the Black Ox". When once the normal form has been attained, or any hypothetical form which stands in parental relation to a group of versions, one can discuss its origins, prehistory, and history. Since the "Black Ox" resembles all other tales in its protean variety, we can profitably discuss only some standardization which represents elements apparently essential to the narrative at a particular time or in a particular region. In some definable relation to this standardized abstraction will stand all forms of the tale. If versions were abundant enough and patience long enough, one might pursue each thread in the strand and show how, when, why, and in what locality it became interwoven with the strand. This task we shall not undertake and the materials for its prosecution have been stored up in the footnotes.

In undertaking the reconstruction we shall examine in turn each incident or trait and seek to establish by comparison its primitive form. After establishing each element in this manner, we may by simple addition of the elements arrive at the outlines of the primitive form of the whole. Each trait will of necessity be either preserved or altered in the process of oral transmission. In the event of its preservation there will of course be no difficulty in the selection of the primitive form, for there is but one to choose. When, however, the episode has been modified in tradition, all its variations, — including of course its absence, which may represent the original situation, — must be collected and examined. These variations will fall into larger and smaller groups and often some will stand quite alone without parallels. Out of these variations it is necessary to select one which exists among them, or to deduce one which is implied by them, as the primitive form. Such a form will not only justify itself as the original, but will also be the basis for explaining the later and varying forms as plausible alterations of the original. Its establishment is the first goal of our efforts, and by its establishment we shall learn much about the origin and dissemination of the tale.

Often, perhaps ordinarily, it is not possible to fix upon the primitive form so directly. Rather the comparison of the variations will lead to the establishment of a local "normal form" which reveals the development of the tale in a particular country or age and which leaves to one side certain recalcitrant and apparently anomalous variations. Yet such recalcitrant variations are likely to be of the utmost importance. When, for example, a story of foreign origin has gained a firm footing in the national stock of narrative, the primitive form will ordinarily have undergone considerable change. The primitive form, if it has maintained itself at all in the competition of new and old, will be represented only by scattering texts which do not fit readily into a scheme. An explanation looking toward their classification as later improvements or corruptions will not be readily discoverable, inasmuch as the significance of such scattering, unclassified texts only becomes evident from the study of versions from other lands or ages. The comparison of the variations within a single episode will therefore determine a "normal form" for the country under discussion and will distinguish certain traits which, because of their peculiar characteristics, may lead, on further study, to a clearer understanding of the tale's history. It is understood of course that the comparison should begin with the versions supplied by one country, and only gradually extend its scope to bring in all the versions available. Only by so restricting the area can the enormous freedom of variation be controlled. In a single region a tale will enter into only a relatively small number of combinations and consequently it will be possible to define with some exactness the elements which can be properly regarded as constituting the tale. When the tale is once defined in this fashion and when the accidental variations are identified and eliminated, then and only then can the tale be studied effectively.

There are various criteria by which a trait is recognized as belonging to the normal or the primitive form. A trait which appears in *many* variants is likely to be old and to be intimately associated with the tale. A trait's *wide distribution* weighs heavily in its favor. Very significant, too, is the *nature of the text* in which the trait occurs: one will give more weight to a trait vouched for by well preserved, carefully told narratives and less weight to a trait found only in narratives which are fragmentary or otherwise known to be corrupt or contaminated. If a trait is *demonstrably old* (either because it occurs in an early version or because it implies ancient custom or superstition), it belongs all the more probably to an early form of the tale. A trait *useful in the management of the story* is very likely to have been long associated with the story and if it is an addition, evidence will usually show where and why — more rarely when — it entered the story. The *readiness with which the varying traits may be derived* from the one selected as primitive or normal may give a further indication of an earlier state of affairs, particularly when such a derivation points to development in one direction and cannot be readily construed in a reverse sense. The establishment of successive traits has a *cumulative* effect: those later established confirm the earlier, or by failing to confirm them, give warning that an error has been made.

Hostile criticisms of method deal largely with these criteria and unfortunately more with their formulation as generalizations than with their specific application. Let it be granted at once that a numerical preponderance of a particular trait among the variations does not establish its position in an earlier hypothetical form. Similarly no single criterion affords a compelling reason for the determination of a trait as primitive. The most determinedly hostile critic must, however, concede that a trait which is widely distributed, which appears frequently in the variants, particularly in the fuller and better ones, which is attested at an early period in the tale's recorded history, which is *per se* old (involving some ancient religious or superstitious idea), which is useful in the tale's economy, which permits competing forms to be derived from it by some natural and readily explicable alteration or substitution, which yields evidence in agreement with that deducible from other traits, and which shows a development in accord with a known or a probable cultural trend, *must* belong to the earliest ascertainable form of the tale. I insist upon the word *must*. Granted that the trait meets these requirements, one is *compelled* to accept it as original; no option is conceivable. But such a fortunate conjuncture is relatively infrequent. From this infrequency arise difficulties which may possibly in any particular instance prove insuperable: the available variants may be insufficiently representative of the tale's distribution or age or may not lend themselves to derivation from a single form, and so on.[1] If all the possible defects

---

[1] In the event that the form deduced as primitive or normal leads to conclusions in disagreement with those implied by other

are present in the evidence, no conclusion can be reached. But such an impasse is also relatively infrequent, at least when the material is sufficiently abundant and the trait important for the conduct of the story. Ordinarily the evidence is defective, inconclusive, or apparently conflicting in one or several regards. We are then confronted with the necessity of scrutinizing each bit of testimony to determine its relative value. Has trait A, which is more widely distributed, a better claim to a place in the normal or the primitive form than trait B, which is reported in greater numbers? To such questions no categorical answer is possible. On one occasion we may select the more widely distributed form of the trait; on another, the more abundantly attested. In either case the choice must be supported by external and persuasive evidence, since a single criterion rarely, if ever, provides a sufficient basis for reaching a decision.

Since the vast bulk of available material in the field of popular tradition belongs to the nineteenth century, efforts to attain to an earlier form of the trait or tale might seem foredoomed to failure. Nevertheless, the situation is not hopeless. Such modern versions afford many instances of traits appearing in two or more forms. Each form may conceivably be equally well attested and may possess, superficially, equal claims to inclusion in a hypothetical earlier form. Yet it is usually possible to make a distinction between them in favor of one particular trait. Since we know what changes can occur in the transmission of tales and how these changes can be used to fix the direction of a tale's development (although as a general principle the change may be from B to A as well as from A to B), we can often identify one form as original and another as

---

traits, some error obviously exists in deduction or interpretation. This constant check on the results is the most valuable and convincing demonstration of the procedure's validity.

secondary. A list of these possible changes was first given by Professor Kaarle Krohn nearly forty years ago,[1] and although the list has been rewritten by Antti Aarne[2] and by Professor Krohn himself,[3] there exists no better brief description of these changes than this first listing, which I give in free translation: "*All the modifications in the motley structure of märchen have arisen in accord with definite laws of thought and fantasy. Among these far from numerous laws may be mentioned: the forgetting of a detail, the acclimatizing of a strange and the modernizing of an obsolete object* [trait], *the generalizing of a special term and the specializing of a general one, the rearranging of the order of events, the confusing of persons or acts, the multiplying, particularly by the numbers 3, 5, and 7* [of persons or things], *polyzoism, in which many animals replace a single one, anthropomorphism of animals and its opposite, egomorphism, in which the narrator himself appears as hero, and so on.*"
With this knowledge of the conditions determining the life of traditional materials, it is ordinarily possible to identify secondary or derivative traits and to select those more primitive ones which yielded later forms. Of course the tabulation must include those versions in which the trait is absent. It is not sufficient to list merely the substitutions and alterations in a trait, for non-existence is itself a variation always to be taken into account. The selection of the primitive trait need not be made from the actually existent variations of the trait, it may also have regard for those implied by or deducible from existent traditional forms. The student must not deny the axiomatic truth of this

---

[1] *Mann uud Fuchs*, Helsingfors, 1891, pp. 8—9. Noteworthy is the omission of contamination, the influence exerted on a tale by analogous tales. — [2] *Leitfaden der vergleichenden Märchenforschung* (FF Comm. 13), pp. 23—39. — [3] *Die folkloristische Arbeitsmethode*, Oslo, 1926, pp. 59—100.

assertion, for the original form (primitive or normal, as the case may be) is either (1) contained in the material collected, or (2) deducible therefrom, or (3) neither contained therein nor deducible therefrom. If the third proposition be maintained, no conclusion whatsoever about the story can be reached. If the evidence permits of no deductions, we must content ourselves with a "non possumus".

It is important to note just what can be accomplished and where the limitations on further progress make themselves felt. Given a sufficient number of versions of the same theme from one cultural area, the manner of its dissemination throughout that area can ordinarily be determined and the changes which have been introduced can be identified. With the addition of outlying versions to the stock it becomes possible to discern the extent to which a tale is of foreign origin and invention or of local, national creation and to establish the country from which it came. When a story of ultimately foreign origin has been substantially recreated in its new home and has established itself in the national narrative stock, the original form, if it has continued to exist at all, will be represented only by texts which do not fit easily into the national pattern. Consequently all variations must be scrutinized with the utmost care, for in some one of them may be concealed a form older than the form which is generally current. Indeed, it is not impossible that the original trait may even then be overlooked. To obtain dependable results one must compare not only a sufficient number of versions to eliminate accidental or intentional alterations and to identify those constituents which cannot be rejected as accidental or intentional alterations but also, in addition to this number, as many versions as may be available from each district in which the tale is current.

The existence of intentional variations in tales is not to be denied for a moment. Indeed, it is impossible to make a distinction between accidental and intentional variations which will serve any useful purpose. But for the moment we may consider those changes which most clearly arise from the originality and inventiveness of a particular narrator. Given a handful of versions, it is usually entirely out of the question to determine what portions are truly characteristic of the tale at a particular stage in its development and what portions are alterations, substitutions, and enlargements of whatever nature. And when the problem is set us in such a form, it often displays an additional and insuperable complication in the fact that the scanty stock of materials represents half a dozen lands and epochs. Occasionally, of course, one can remove without difficulty the additions of a particular age (e.g. the mythological costume of the Latin Cupid and Psyche, the allegorical elements of an animal tale, or the Arthurian additions to a fairy tale) or the alterations to accomodate it to a particular literary form. But when we possess a generous supply of materials, the identification of intentional modifications is easy. As simple an example as any is the shifting of the narrative from the third to the first person or vice verse. Had we only a few texts and those widely separated in time and space, it might readily be impossible to discover the original form. With two or three score texts from a relatively narrow area the chances of success are enormously increased. The reader will perhaps be inclined to think that the recognition of intentional and purposeful alterations offers serious difficulties, but in the main it does not. Of course as soon as a change is perceived to be intentional, it can be disposed of. Furthermore, the reader may be inclined to think that intentional changes of a subversive sort are frequent. In fact, such changes are rare. The variation in traditional materials is relatively continuous over an area within which a gradual drift in one direction can ordinarily be recognized. Subversive changes are likely to create a new form, which has then a history and a dissemination of its own.

A much more troublesome problem appears in the recognition of tales influenced by or derived from standard collections, notably from the Grimms' *Kinder- und Hausmärchen,* which have undergone a process of "improvement" more or less in keeping with the spirit of the folk. It is often practically impossible to discover whether a particular version, collected from an oral source, is one of the *Kinder- und Hausmärchen* which has undergone change and adaptation in the course of oral transmission or whether it is representative of popular tradition and has suffered from contamination with the *Kinder- und Hausmärchen.* So far as the individual version is concerned, the determination of the point is of interest. So far as the course of an investigation is concerned, the matter can usually be neglected, if the texts are sufficiently abundant. A tale which has been clearly recognized to be related in one way or another to a printed collection can scarcely afford any information of crucial importance.

The procedure accomplishes the following result: it tabulates the evidence from which a selection must be made, it forces upon us the necessity of reaching a decision, it employs logical means to that end, it provides at each stage the opportunity to question the decision reached,[1] and deductions as to origin and dissemination may follow then as a consequence. Its novelty lies wholly, as I see it, in combining two notions, neither of which is new or strange:

---

[1] The advantage of this opportunity may seem small, but it will be immediately evident to one who reads an essay by Benfey or Cosquin, to mention only two of the greatest names. This method makes it possible to put one's finger instantly on the flaw in the reasoning. See, e.g., Krohn's incisive criticism of Mackensen's study; it will be found in *Die folkloristische Arbeitsmethode,* pp. 133 ff.

the recognition and definition of criteria by which the primitive or normal form of a tale can be established and the employment of a systematic knowledge of the possible changes which may occur in a trait. As Kipling has said, there are ninety-nine ways of making a tribal lay and every one of them is right. The obvious corollary to this is: If one knows the ninety-nine ways and identifies the development in a special case as conforming to a particular way, one has found a plausible and reasonable explanation of the development. And since a particular one of the ninety-nine ways will ordinarily afford a better explanation than the others, the temptation to accept the explanation as correct is strong indeed. The corollary is not, as Kipling meant to imply, that there is no hope of settling anything. Furthermore, if a proposed explanation involves a hundredth way, i.e. an explanation which conflicts with what we know to be the rules of traditional materials, its complete rejection must follow instantly on discovery of the fact.[1]

The determination of the original trait by comparison of the variations among the versions is not all that must be done. For a simple story the assembling of the original traits, as they have been established, will yield a sufficiently good approximation to an original tale. But the whole is always something more than the combination of its parts and such a purely mechanical assembling can give no more than a sketch, an outline of the original tale. Some additions and corrections can be made as soon as the assembling is complete, for then the gaps will be most apparent. In some matters the need for correction may be evident, although a wholly satisfying cure may be impossible. General principles touching the structure of

---

[1] See an effort to show an instance of this sort in the articles of C. W. von Sydow and Finnur Jónsson in *Folkminnen och Folktankar*, VIII (1921), 75 ff., 129 ff., 132 ff.

popular tradition can be invoked, although such principles have not yet been thoroughly worked out.[1] Some general principles may give standards by which to judge the product of the reassembling. Concerning the main structural outlines of the prototypic tales we are not as yet very well informed, although we seem to be coming to the conclusion that the older tales were relatively simple and composed of few incidents.[2] A corollary to this conclusion is that the European stock of tales is the result of riotous interchange and entanglement.

As a matter of fact, some feeling of uncertainty necessarily inheres in the end-product of this or of any reconstruction. The useful result lies primarily in the discovery of the tale's history, and the procedure seems logically sound so far as this is concerned. The "original tale" is an abstraction on which it is dangerous to base far-reaching deductions, and it may be fairly compared to the chemist's atom or the famous "benzene ring" of organic chemistry. No one disputes the results obtained by the use of these concepts, although the concepts themselves are far from established as physical facts. In the present case it will be seen that the versions which stand near the beginning of the tale's life-history could in no way have been deduced *in full* from the later versions. The outlines can be made out, but the major differences could never have been disco-

---

[1] The most important studies are A. van Gennep, *La formation des légendes*, Paris, 1917; Axel Olrik, *Nogle Grundsætninger for Sagnforskning* (Danmarks Folkeminder 23), Copenhagen, 1921 (and the very considerable literature regarding the "epic laws"; see Olrik, p. 66); W. A. Berendsohn, *Grundformen volkstümlicher Erzählerkunst in den Kinder- und Hausmärchen der Brüder Grimm*, Hamburg, 1922. The brief sketch in Krohn, *Die folkloristische Arbeitsmethode*, pp. 100 ff. gives some suggestive applications. —
[2] See, e.g., C. W. von Sydow, "Folksagan såsom indoeuropeisk tradition", *Arkiv for nordisk filologi*, XLII (1925—26), 1—17 and the references in the previous note.

vered by any union of searching analysis and subsequent synthesis. Similarly John Meier has shown that there is no reasonable chance, indeed no chance whatsoever, of recovering the literary song *(Kunstlied)* which has yielded a popular song *(volkstümliches Lied)* by a comparison of versions taken from oral circulation.[1] *Certain elements of the original form can be established and the course of development can be defined, but more is beyond our powers.*

One of the commonest versions of the tale which we are to study is the following:

When he is plowing, a farmer throws a knife into a whirlwind, for he had heard that this causes the whirlwind to disappear. A Lapp orders him to come after his knife or all will not be well. The farmer arrives Christmas eve. While eating, he sees his knife and recognizes it. He wants to return for the holiday dinner. The Lapp promises to take him for the ox that stands at the door-post. The Lapp says, "Will you go like thought, like a bullet, or like a black cock?" The farmer answers, "Like a black cock." He is put in a trough dawn by reindeer. The trough bumps into a steeple. The farmer's cap flies off, but it is not recovered, for it lies 500 km. behind. At home the farmer orders the maid to substitute a smaller black ox. But the Lapp and the ox are in the trough and the bellowing of the ox is audible as they disappear.[2]

---

[1] *Kunstlieder im Volksmunde,* Halle a. S., 1906, p. XXXII. —
[2] This story will be found in the appended tabulation of versions under the identifying mark b 8. To each story is assigned a letter designating the particular region of Finland in which it was recovered and a number indicating its sequence. The choice of letters was made by Kaarle Krohn in his publications of the variants of Finnish folktales, and is generally used for these purposes by Finnish scholars. See, e.g., Kaarle Krohn, *Die folkloristische Arbeitsmethode,* Oslo, 1926, pp. 50 ff. In the present instance the letter b signifies the district of Satakunta in southwestern Finland and the number 8 indicates that seven other

Of this story more than a hundred versions have been taken down in Finland; these are available to us in the archives of the Finnish Literary Society (Suomalaisen Kirjallisuuden Seura) in Helsingfors. For the reader's convenience abstracts in which no trait or detail is intentionally omitted are printed at the end of the present study. In fact, no study of tradional materials should be issued in which the evidence is not thus fully presented for the reader's inspection.[1] The following study will examine one by one the different traits of the tale and will endeavor to discover as far as may be possible the oldest or the original form in each instance. The general principles of this procedure have already been explained in the introduction, and we may now undertake their application in specific instances.

A farmer.

Between "man" and "farmer" it is impossible to make a distinction, so far as this story is concerned. Since the man owned cattle, as appears from the later course of the tale, we may call him a farmer without more ado. A listing of the instances in which the hero is called either "man" or "farmer" will not be instructive or useful. The only instances which need to be remarked upon are those in which something contradictory or additional is mentioned.

---

versions from this region occur in the index of variants before this one. In the following discussion reference to the individual versions will be made solely by this method, and the reader is urged to verify each mention of a tale by the tabulation of abstracts at the end of the study. — [1] Aarne's remarks *(Leitfaden der vergleichenden Märchenforschung, FF Comm.* 13, p. 78) on this point are easily misconstrued. Certainly the reader is entitled to know more than only those traits which are mentioned in the study.

In two texts the hero is a sailor (FS[1] taken down on the seacoast) or a fisherman, who, however, owns a few cows (b 6). The cattle, which are necessary to the story, have been retained, while the vocation of the hero has been adapted, in the special locale, to the trade most familiar or most interesting to the narrator. The figures of the sailor and the fisherman are to be rejected: they cannot preserve a recollection of an earlier form. Their rejection is based on several grounds: (1) scarcity of instances; (2) inappropriateness to the story; (3) occurrence in versions which are evidently corrupt and confused (for neither FS nor b 6 can be considered well told, particularly in the introductory episodes); (4) existence of a plausible reason for the change; (5) restricted distribution. The last of these needs perhaps a word of explanation. If the version containing the sailor had been recorded in central Finland, far from the coast or any relation to the sea, such a version might have been considered a relic of any early form which had been preserved only in that region, while elsewhere the tale had been altered. A trait which does not accord with the cultural background of its place of origin affords indubitable evidence of the tale's transmission and consequently implies the existence of at least one stage earlier than the one in hand.

There are, furthermore, a few other similar instances of casual local adaptation to the narrator's interests. Thus two versions (a 1, b 2) make the hero a hired man. Since the resulting difficulty about the ox, which a hired man could not be expected to own, is resolved in two different ways, viz., no explanation is given as to the ownership of the ox (b 2) or the whole episode of transportation and reward, in which alone the ox is necessary, is absent

---

[1] This abbreviation refers to the one Finnish tale recorded in Swedish: it will be found in the tabulated abstracts.

(a 1), and since neither of these sadly defective forms can be original or representative, the hired man can make no claim to inclusion in a hypothetical earlier tale.

In those three versions [1] in which the hero is said to be a "Finn", he is also a farmer. The hero's nationality has nothing to do with the story, while his vocation has considerable significance. The antithesis of Finn and Lapp, which is familiar in Finnish life, is implied in the story, but cannot have made part of the normal form. The specific mention of the "Finn" is therefore to be rejected. The reader will note that those versions which mention the "Finn" are from east Finnish sources, but the fact cannot be used to draw any conclusions regarding the accuracy of east Finnish tradition as compared with west Finnish. With these observations in mind we conclude that the hero was a farmer; he was not a seaman, fisherman, or hired man, and he was not declared to be of specifically Finnish nationality.

Those tales in which the farmer is named or in which the scene is fixed or in which the time of the action is given represent efforts to give the tale a local habitation. [2] Such traits are perhaps not to be assigned to the normal form, but in the matter a positive decision is out of the question. C. W. von Sydow's assertion that the older forms of popular narrative were furnished with names and dates may well be borne out by this evidence. [3] In any event, it is now impossible to recover the details.

---

[1] f 9; j 8; l 1; cf. a 1, "Finnish laborer". — [2] a 2, 5; b 2, 3, 5, 7, 10; e 1, 3—4; f 2, 3, 6; g 4, 6; i 1—4; j 1, 6, 15; l 4, 11; m 1, 2, 4—6; s 1. Farmers from named parishes: d 3; e 2, 7; f 3, 10; g 8; j 13; k 6. Dating of the tale: b 2 (in the seventeenth century); e 1 (three generations before); i 4 (five generations before); m 1, 2 (300 years ago). — [3] "Folksagan såsom indoeuropeisk tradition", *Arkiv for nordisk filologi*, XLII (1925—26), 1—17.

Who is haying.[1]

Concerning this unimportant point the evidence is not abundant. Yet the discussion will bring out clearly the nature of a geographical limitation on a trait. "Harvesting", which occurs but once (l 2), is a generalization not to be distinguished from haying. "Out of doors" (k 3) is a simplification. Specialization is seen in certain instances in which the farmer is eating while the whirlwind passes[2] or is cutting his nails, while threshing corn (a 5).[3] In the last the reminiscence of the normal form is obvious.

A seasonal change which has acquired some currency seems secondary in origin: the farmer is sowing barley,[4] or rye,[5] or plowing,[6] or burning stumps preparatory to plowing.[7] The last is a pretty example of a narrator's embellishment. "Working in a field"[8] is a generalized form and evidently dependent on "plowing", — note the fact that the wind raises dust.

Since the trait of the "haying" is not widely attested, one hesitates to accept it.[9] The distribution, furthermore, is very curious, for the trait is limited to the four west Finnish districts (a, b, d, k), with the exceptions of g 2 and l 2. Such a minor detail as this does not occur often enough in the available material to provide a foundation for any conclusion, and we must avoid reaching a conclusion based on meagre evidence. A decision, — which is here anticipated by the inclusion of the trait in the nor-

---

[1] a 2, 8; b 4, 5, 13; d 2, 5; k 1, 2. — [2] a 3; b 4, 6. — [3] The episode appears to have some connection with a later one, in which eating plays an important part. The episode in these two forms supplies here an excuse for the farmer's having the knife ready to throw. — [4] a 6, cf. b 10. — [5] b 3. — [6] b 2, b 8, cf. b 10. — [7] g 2. — [8] b 10. — [9] Strong confirmatory evidence may, however, be found in those tales in which a farmer throws a knife at a whirlwind, since many such tales declare that the farmer was haying. For references see the note on p. 25.

mal form, — will only be possible when, as a result of the discussion immediately following, we are quite clear about the larger narrative element to which this trait of the haying belongs. Yet our attention is already drawn to one fact of importance: a sharp contrast exists between east and west Finnish tradition.

Throws a knife at a passing whirlwind.[1]

The distribution of this trait is curiously limited: the four western districts (a, b, d, k)[2] show a marked predilection for it. In a (Finland proper) no other form is known, in b (Satakunta) and k (South Österbotten) another form is recorded but once in 13 and 6 times respectively, and finally in d (South and Middle Tavastland) the versions are equally divided between two forms, one with the whirlwind and one without. Furthermore, the trait of the whirlwind occurs once in almost all the eastern districts (f, g, j, l, m). In brief, the trait of the whirlwind is firmly established in west Finnish tradition, and is found sporadically

---

[1] a 2—9; b 1—6, 8—13; c 1; d 2, 5, 6; f 9; g 2; j 12; k 1—3, 5, 6; l 2; m 1; cf. E 1. Those few texts which have another object than a whirlwind are clearly derivative in nature: a torch (k 6); birds (b 6). Both versions are deformed in other respects, especially b 6. The one version (a 1) in which the Lapp throws the knife is hopelessly distorted. His swearing (which is mentioned in a 5, 6; b 2, 10, 13; k 2; and which gives rise to corrupted forms in a 7, 8) is a trait associated with supernatural creatures; cf. e.g. J. Grimm, *Deutsche Mythologie*[4], III, 452, No. 522. Whether the swearing belongs to the story is wholly uncertain. Its appearance in a (Finland proper) seems to betoken the age of the tradition preserved in that district. — [2] From the fifth western district (c: Nyland) only one version is reported, and its relation to the group of tales before us is dubious.

in east Finnish tradition. The situation in Finland can be presented most clearly by a diagram:

Whirlwind:

	1	1	
5	—	1	1
12	3	1	—
8	(1)		

No mention:

	11	5	
1	9	7	14
1	3	9	5
—	—		

Let us turn to the many versions[1] which contain no mention of the whirlwind; perhaps it will be possible to discover whether the trait of the whirlwind was originally part of the story or not. A number of these versions can be rejected as possessing no evidential value, e.g., those which may not belong to the cycle of the Black Ox at all,[2] and which are in any event much corrupted. In many instances the omission might conceivably be due to hasty recording by our informant; compare e.g., such a version as e 6, which contains no more than the following: "To Lapland. Black ox." Yet, even after the exclusion of abbreviated and unduly condensed versions, — a procedure which is naturally more or less subjective and therefore does not lend itself to tabulation, — a considerable number of versions remain in which such an explanation is impossible. The existence of a form of the story in which the whirlwind does not appear must be recognized.

The distribution of those versions in which the whirlwind is absent is significant. They occur almost solely in eastern Finland and northern Tavastland (e), which was settled by emigrants from eastern Finland (i.e., in the districts

---

[1] b 7; d 1, 3, 4; e 1—9; f 1—8, 10; g 1, 3—8; i 1—5; j 1—11, 13—15; k 4; l 1, 3—12; m 2—6. — [2] a 1; c 1; k 6.

known as e, f, g, i, j, l, m). Our particular attention is attracted to the five west Finnish instances.[1] In one of these (k 4) a probable, nay almost certain reminiscence of the whirlwind appears later in the story: the farmer returns in a whirlwind.[2] The version d 3 is brief and lacks some very characteristic incidents of the story, in particular the episode of the ox paid by the farmer for the trip. Whether d 3 belongs to the cycle of the Black Ox is more or less uncertain; in any event it cannot be regarded as a well-told version, if it is assigned to the cycle. The remaining versions[3] conform closely to the east Finnish type.

As a consequence of the divergence in the versions we have to decide at the very beginning of our study what constitutes the story.[4] This might seem a very simple question indeed, one so simple that the answer was self-evident, but a reading of the list of versions makes it clear that the question cannot be answered offhand. In the present case, is the whirlwind episode inserted in the western versions or omitted in the eastern ones? A decision in this important question will be likely to fix the direction in which the story has travelled. Yet the possibility of an erroneous decision need not deter us, for opportunities to correct such a mistake will present themselves again and again. If the evidence obtained in the determination of all the episodes marks out the same line of transmission, its cumulative weight will carry conviction. The conviction will be due to the fact that the result obtained in one instance is, so far as the reasoning and evidence are concerned, altogether independent of any other instance. If

---

[1] b 7; d 1, 3, 4; k 4. For the reason given in the text, k 4 is omitted in all later consideration of this group. — [2] See also b 12, f 6, and compare k 1. — [3] b 7; d 1, d 4. — [4] Bédier (*Les fabliaux*², p. 187) ignores this difficulty completely. His determination of what constitutes the substance of the story is wholly arbitrary.

the conclusion baesd on one episode conflicts with that from another, we shall have to re-examine the conclusions in both cases.

Two possible means of attack on the difficulty presented by the conflict in tradition suggest themselves. If the whirlwind episode has been omitted by eastern narrators, there may yet remain traces of its former presence and of its significance in the story. If it has been added to the western versions, we may hope to find some instances in which the joint is still apparent. Ordinarily it will be easier to discover traces of a lost episode, if any exist, than signs of a juncture. Traces of a lost episode may appear in even the most fragmentary version while a joining will ordinarily be discernible only in a relatively complete and carefully told form. For this reason let us look for traces of the whirlwind episode in eastern tradition. Such traces exist in some widely dispersed versions,[1] which differ among themselves very considerably. As chance has it, the number of these texts approximates that of the west Finnish versions which exhibit the east Finnish form of the story. Consequently any argument from numerical preponderance, as regards either the total number of versions or the number of exceptions, goes by the board.

The area of a trait's distribution may give some indication of its normal form. At first glance the distribution of the two forms seems to give no indication of an earlier state of affairs: the western form is current in several eastern districts, while the eastern form is as widely current in the west. Superficially honors appear to be even. Yet a glance at the diagram shows that the western form enjoys a much wider distribution. Furthermore, an examination of

---

[1] g 2; m 1. The knife in f 9 belongs ultimately to the knife which appears in the whirlwind episode. On the importance of the versions j 12 and l 2 see below.

the west Finnish instances of the eastern form discloses that they are all from regions immediately adjoining the east Finnish districts and that they are all closely related, since all contain the incident of the rider striking the church or losing his hat. On the other hand, the east Finnish instances of the western form, i.e. those east Finnish tales in which the episode of the whirlwind occurs, are found in regions far from geographical contact with west Finnish tradition and differ much among themselves. The differences suggest that these east Finnish tales of the west Finnish form have been established in tradition for some time and have maintained themselves independently on east Finnish soil, while the close connection of the opposed group of tales implies a more recent origin. The geographical situation may be described as follows: The east Finnish form (whirlwind lacking) makes itself felt on the eastern edge of the area within which the west Finnish tale is known. Although the west Finnish form (whirlwind present) begins to yield ground in d (South and Middle Tavastland), the easternmost of the west Finnish districts, its influence extends into the easternmost regions of the east Finnish districts. The answer to the question with which we are inmediately concerned is implied in such a summary: the tale has passed from west Finland to east Finland and in so doing has lost the episode of the whirlwind.

But before accepting this conclusion let us see whether any criteria other than that of geographical distribution will bear it out. The episode of the whirlwind is ancient, for it involves a belief in the power of demons to travel in whirlwinds, a belief which bot his old and widely disseminated.[1]

---

[1] See Feilberg, *Bidrag till en ordbog over jyske Almuesmål*, I, 787; IV (Tillæg), 232 *(s.v. hvirvelvind);* and cf. further J. Grimm, *Deutsche Mythologie*[4], III, 452, No. 522; L. von Schroeder, "Germanische Elben und Götter beim Estenvolke", *Sitz. ber.* (phil.-hist. Kl.), Vienna, CLIII (1906), No. 1, p. 9, n. 3, cf. p. 31, n. 4;

More than this, the very incident which we are discussing exists as an independent story in popular tradition. It is very widely disseminated and a Danish instance, which will serve for many others, is as follows:

A man in Africa flies to Europe in a whirlwind. A turf-digger draws his knife, throws it into the whirlwind, and loses sight of it. Later the turf-digger becomes a soldier, is captured, and is taken to Africa. There he meets a lame man and sees his own knife on the table. He claims the knife and learns that it has injured his host.[1]

Clearly the mythical notion of demons traveling in whirlwinds has been in existence long enough to form part of any hypothetical form we may care to create, and it is quite clear, too, that the Finnish tale of the "Black Ox" has employed narrative materials already shaped by tradition. The existence in Finland of such materials is attested by our versions a 3, c 1, d 5. No one, I suppose, will claim for a moment that the Danish tale and its analogues are fragments of the "Black Ox", and should any one do so, a glance at the versions of the theme, which differ

---

J. Aubrey, *Miscellanies* (1696), p. 123; J. Skar, *Gamalt ur Sætesdal*, II, 48; Ilwof, *Zs. d. Ver. f. Vk.*, VII (1897), 189; Bulmer, *J. Am. Fl.*, VII (1894), 156; P. S[ébillot], *Rev. des tr. pop.*, VI (1891), 549; Sébillot, *Folklore de France*, I, 82, 113; *Gent. Mag. Lib.*, IV, 4, 41 f.; J. G. Campbell, *Superstitions*, pp. 24, 25, 87, 88; *Athenaeum* (London), 1847, p. 17; Lady Wilde, *Anc. Leg.*, I, 243; *Mitt. jüd. Vk.*, I (1898), 70; "Lageniensis", *Irish Folk-Lore*, p. 34; B. Hunt, *Folktales of Breffny*, p. 71; Wentz, *Fairy Faith*, p. 51: *Folk-Lore*, IV (1893), 351; XVI (1905), 177; *Scottish Hist. Rev.*, VII, 365; *Journ. Cork Hist. and Arch. Soc.*, n.s. II, 318. — [1] Kristensen, *Danske Sagn*, II, 140, No. 150. See in general Feilberg, *Bidrag*, I, 707 (hvirvelvind), IV, 232; E. H. Meyer, *Germanische Mythologie* (1891), p. 137, § 175; L. v Schroeder "Germanische Elben u. Götter bein Estenvolke", *Sitzungsberichte* (phil.-hist. Klasse), Vienna, CLIII (1906), No. 1, p. 31 n. 4; Sébillot, *Folklore de France*, I, 113; Laistner, *Rätsel der Sphinx*, I, 109, 162, 165, 234, II, 110, 197; Holmberg, *Die Religion der Tscheremissen*, FFC 61, p. 54, n. 1.

enormously among themselves, will convince him that the Danish tale represents a very old semi-mythical tale. It is obvious that we are dealing with a component of the "Black Ox" and not with a fragment split off from it.

Is the episode of the whirlwind essential to the "Black Ox"? To this question the answer is affirmative, for inasmuch as the episode is after the manner of an explanation — it tells why the farmer made the trip to Lapland —, it is particularly subject to the dangers of loss, contraction, or substitution. Explanations of actions and reasons for them are particularly exposed to mutilation and deformation. Those versions in which the narrative begins with a bald statement of the farmer's illness, e.g., g 8: "Man from Kuopio had been to Lapland to be cured", or this more striking instance (j 1): "Karvinen, who was struck by an evil spirit, is taken to Lapland for cure", need more explanation of the illness or of the spirit's anger than the narrator grants us. But a full discussion of the reason for the journey must be reserved for the next section.

The conclusion is, therefore, that the whirlwind episode is to be assigned to the normal form. The deduction which follows at once is that the tale shows a progressive deterioration from west to east and that consequently the tale was transmitted from west to east. This deduction agrees with the trend of cultural currents in Finland.

A word regarding the short and seemingly corrupt versions will be in place. These are not all to be thrown together without further consideration. Some short versions are probably contractions and corruptions, e. g., d 3, in which the mention of Nastola church suggests the comparison of such versions as b 9 where the church has an important function in the story. The deficiencies of such versions as e 4, 6, 7, 8 are to be laid at the door of the narrator or recorder. Other versions have on the contrary an entirely different look; thus a 3, c 1, and d 5 are, as we have seen, narratives allied to the "Black Ox" rather than versions of it. They are not corrupt or defective in the same sense that the former class of versions is and indeed the terms "corrupt" and "defective" should not be applied to them at all.

He goes to Lapland.[1]

The predominance of this trait in Finnish tradition establishes its place in the normal form; whether it is the original trait remains to be seen. A conclusion can be reached only by study of the variant forms of the trait. Occasionally a characteristic detail is underscored: Breadless Lapland,[2] Fire Lapland,[3] a parish in northern Lapland.[4] In the various instances there is but the name of Lapland in common and each variation is strictly limited in its distribution. Consequently these variations are most readily explained as embellishments of the normal form, for the addition of such details is quite in keeping with the natural wish of the narrator to enlarge upon his story. It is conceivable that Petrograd (f 8) and Stockholm (FS) are chance modifications of a similar sort. Such scenes have no real appropriateness to the story, while the symbolism of Lapland is fundamental. But this decision cannot be insisted upon and will be confirmed or overthrown by examination of versions from outside of Finland. In the same way the island in k 1 may be a substitute for Lapland, since the farmer finds a Lapp in a hut on the island. But concerning these three texts[5] more will be said later.

Some versions have developed in an opposite direction; instead of introducing a special feature, which has perhaps no significant application, they have substituted vague and

---
[1] a 1, 2, 5, ,7; b 2, 3, 5—13; d 1—4, 6; e 1—9; f 1—7, 9, 10; g 1—8; i 1—5; j 1—4, 6, 8—15; k 2—7; l 1, 2, 4—6, 8—10, 12; m 1—6; s 1; E 1. — [2] b 2, 9. — [3] i 3—5. — [4] f10. — [5] f 8; k 1; FS.

colorless generalities. Thus certain versions specify no place,[1] or one which is meaningless: "on a journey",[2] "very far from home",[3] or "a farm".[4] In a most corrupt version,[5] if it is indeed a version of the "Black Ox", the hero does not leave home, and, since there is no mention of the ox, the whole falls to the ground. Such imperfect versions can afford no safe basis for deductions about the normal or primitive form.

We therefore conclude that the goal of the journey is Lapland in the normal form, and Lapland without any modifying adjective. The normal form is, to be sure, no bald schema, it has vitality, vigor, and characteristic detail; but descriptive adjectives concerning Lapland are so infrequent, so limited in distribution, and so readily explained as merely local enlargements that we are not justified in considering them relics of an earlier form.

There remain those variations which make the end of the journey a demon's[6] or a wizard's[7] house, a not entirely canny scene where cursing food is more welcome than blessing it,[8] or a forest to which the hero is carried by devils.[9] Conceivably Lapland, which has a well-established reputation as the land of magic and sorcery, may have been replaced by these paraphrases, and on the basis of the Finnish evidence alone we might be led to such a conclusion. Yet the derivation in this fashion is not entirely convincing and satisfactory, for the trait is rather widely distributed and has a very distinctive form. For the present it will suffice to point out that these variants do not represent the normal Finnish form, which can be explained as an outgrowth, a specialization of these variants. It is also worth noting that in the preliminary tabulation of this trait a visit to Lappish wisemen and a visit to Lapland

---

[1] b 1; l 3, 7, 11. — [2] j 7. — [3] j 5. — [4] a 6. — [5] a 3. — [6] b 4; f 8. — [7] a 5; b 1; d 5; cf. b 2; f 10; g 7. — [8] a 8. — [9] a 9.

have been grouped under the same head. Obviously it is practically impossible to make a distinction in the narratives as they are preserved. But it is conceivable that the visit to the Lappish wisemen is a stage intermediate between the visit to the uncanny farmstead and the visit to Lapland. The trait of the visit to a wizard's house may consequently preserve something ancient, and that fact can be best perceived by comparison with versions from outside Finland. Such a comparison will be undertaken later. The discovery of something which may possibly represent the oldest Finnish form of the narrative is interesting, and more than that, for this discovery confirms the growing impression that the west Finnish versions are superior to the east Finnish. This conclusion has been suggested by the discussion of previous variants, and the weight of cumulative testimony is beginning to tell.

It is interesting to return for a moment to the three versions f 8, k 1; FS. More light falls on f 8: "Man at Petrograd Christmas eve wishes to go home. *Devil* offers to take him . . ." and its near relative j 7: "Man on journey. Kekri near. *Devil* says that if he gives cow . . ." For the devil is seen to be the equivalent of the wizard or the Lapp. Furthermore, it is now clear that the interest in FS, "Finnish sailor in Stockholm Christmas eve. *Lapp* will take him home", and k 1, "Goes to sea in a boat which carries him to an island where there is a Lapp's cabin", turns on the Lapp as a practitioner of magic and not as a resident of Lapland. As a consequence the development may be conceived somewhat as follows: (1) visit to wizard; (2) visit to Lapp magician; (3) visit to Lapp in Lapland. And there are traces of the wizard (ex hypothesi stage 1) in the tales involving Lapland (stage 3).

It will be noticed that no reason for the trip has been assigned. This matter, which has already been touched on, must be investigated, although a decision will be difficult to reach. The remark has previously been made that explanations of acts are particularly likely to suffer change, and this instance is no exception to the rule. In a large number of instances no explanation of the journey is forthcoming.[1] It will at least clear the ground to examine these and show that they preserve no old form. Not much weight can be given to the frequency with which such an explanation is absent, and a critical examination of the list reveals that few versions afford any basis for drawing conclusions.[2] After discarding these, the versions remaining are not impressive in their frequency.[3] Since an obvious explanation for their existence, i. e. carelessness of one kind or another, is available, they need be considered no further. The conclusion, which is inherently reasonable, follows that an explanation for the journey was present in the earlier forms of the tale.

There are four main varieties among the explanations which the versions offer: (1) the farmer is carried to Lapland by a whirlwind; (2) he is forced to come by magic or by conscience; (3) he goes for help in sickness; (4) he seeks counsel. The first of these is restricted to southwestern Finland, where the whirlwind carries the farmer at once to Lapland.[4] Clearly a weakened form is that in which we have the whirlwind, followed by the farmer's departure because he is ordered, conjured, driven by an urgent and

---

[1] a 3; c 1; d 3, 5; e 2—4, 6—8; f 1, 2, 8; g 4, 7; i 4; j 4, 5, 7, 9—11, 13, 14: k 4; l 3—5, 7—9, 11; m 3, 4, 6. — [2] The following unduly abbreviated versions must be omitted: d 3; e 2—4, 6—8; f 1, 2, 8; g 4, 7; i 4; j 4, 5, 7, 9—11, 13, 14; l 3, 5, 7—9, 11; m 3, 4, 6. These cannot be expected to give any reliable information regarding an earlier state of affairs, so far as this point is concerned. Certainly a 3 and c 1, which has no trip to Lapland, have no bearing on the present discussion, for it is doubtful whether they are properly members of the cycle of the Black Ox. — [3] d 5; g 7; k 4. — [4] a 5, 7—9; b 2.

unexplained desire or by conscience, or impelled by a wish to find his knife.[1] Then comes a group in which we have the whirlwind, followed by the farmer's illness.[2] It seems not improbable that the illness of the farmer is connected with the injury to the Lapp and perhaps transferred from it. And lastly, — I anticipate what follows —, we have merely illness or other explanations without the whirlwind. The development is a steady rationalization by removal or replacement of supernatural elements, but the fact that the present instance exemplifies a steady rationalization is not for a moment to be elevated into a general principle that all development is in the direction of rationalization.

In a large number of versions the hero is seized with some ailment, — only rarely as a consequence of throwing the knife at a whirlwind, — and goes to Lapland for cure.[3] The trait is widespread, but characteristically eastern in its distribution. Concerning the exact nature of the ailment we are quite in the dark; there is no agreement among the versions on this point. In b 13 and k 3 the farmer suffers pain in the thigh, a situation which bears out the suggestion made above that the illness has been transferred from the Lapp to the farmer in order to provide a good excuse for the journey to Lapland. Such an excuse

---

[1] Conjured to come to Lapland: b 1, 8, 9; perhaps b 12 (cf. k 1), in which the man goes at once to search for his knife, may find a place here. Compare b 3, 10, and 12 with one another. See a 2, 6; b 3, 5, 6; d 2; k 5 for twinges of conscience. Note j 15, the farmer "is troubled by an evil spirit", and compare it with j 1 and j 2, in which the farmer is flogged by an evil spirit. The last three versions confirm the belief that the original whirlwind episode has been lost, for the whirlwind episode with the knife throwing is the cause of the spirit's anger. See also j 12 and l 2 where the episode of the return is absent. — [2] b 4, 13; g 2; k 2, 3. — [3] See f 3, 9, 10; g 1, 5, 8; j 1, 2, 15; l 1, 2, 6, 10, 12; s 1. Cf. b 7 (his sons are sick) and the disorganized incident in a 1. See also the preceding note.

was all the more necessary since the episode of the whirlwind had been lost. Certainly such explanatory details as the following are caused by a meaningless specializing: epilepsy;[1] chirping of grasshoppers in the ears (s 1).[2]

When the farmer goes to Lapland in search of counsel, we have a weakened or generalized form of trip caused by his illness: in the place of a vaguely remembered illness some other mishap may have entered the story. He goes for advice about poor crops,[3] bad fortune,[4] death of sons and loss of iron arms,[5] loss or death of cattle.[6] The last pair of misfortunes, the loss and death of cattle, is apparently an anticipation of the final episode, the loss of the Black Ox. It will be noticed that the last pair of misfortunes is found only in eastern Finland and evidently represents a special, local development.

Many tales declare simply that the farmer goes to get counsel of an unspecified sort.[7] This may be conceived as a generalized form of the preceding, or it may be brought into direct connection with those tales in which the farmer is forced by his conscience to go to Lapland, which in turn may be a weakened form of compulsion by magic. Those texts in which the farmer makes the trip to obtain mysterious knowledge[8] or to learn witchcraft[9] are therefore open to two explanations, either a trace of the magic element in the compulsion to make the journey has been preserved in the notion of the trip to obtain mysterious knowledge (or to learn witchhraft), or the development has been from the specialized form "sickness" through the generalized "counsel" to the specialized "witchcraft".

---

[1] g 1, 5. — [2] See the remarks in the first note on p. 31: j 1, j 2, and j 15. — [3] b 11; k 6. — [4] d 6; cf. e 1. — [5] b 7. — [6] e 5, e 9; f 4, 6; j 6. — [7] b 7, 11; d 1, 4, 6; e 5, 10; f 4—7; g 3, 6; i 1—3, 5; j 3, 8; k 7; m 1, 2, 5; cf. j 8. — [8] d 1, 4; f 5; g 3; i 1, 5; k 7. — [9] g 6, 7; j 8; m 1.

Obvious developments in the direction of specialization can be seen in the following explanations of the journey: ignorance of the fate of a lost child (i 3), desire to discover who stole a sum of money (f 7) or to find a lucky site for a farm (m 5), to learn how to recover money which has been buried under such severe prohibitions that even the owner cannot raise it (m 2). A curious enlargement by which the trip is doubled occurs in j 3, where two make the trip to Lapland, the one to learn how to kill his neighbor secretly, and the other to learn how to escape being killed.

He sees his own knife in the Lapp's house.[1]

The recognition of the knife certainly belongs in the normal form. Its frequent non-appearance need not be tabulated or examined in detail because it is logically dependent on the whirlwind episode and the loss of the knife. Yet the knife episode has been preserved in two instances in which the related episode has totally disappeared. To be sure, it is preserved in a strangely modified shape, e.g. in e 1: "The Lapp steps out and returns with the knife belonging to Hyytiäinen's wife."[2] A comparable preservation of the knife incident, although in wholly different form, is found in f 9:

> The Lapp shows the knife which the Finn had lost the previous summer while plowing. Then the Lapp brings in a tub of water and tells the Finn to strike a woman in the ribs, when she appears in the water. She has caused the Finn's illness. Although he does not, he is cured.[3]

---

[1] a 3—9; b 1—6, 8—13; d 2, 5, 6; g 2; j 12; k 1—3, 5, 6; l 2; cf. e 1; f 9. — [2] The incident is parallel to that in k 7 in which the Lapp visits the farmer's home and brings back tokens. — [3] Here a new theme is brought into the tale: A person who is being threatened by a magician takes refuge in a tub of water.

Here there is a trace of the knife, although the whirlwind episode, of which the plowing appears to be the only fragment remaining, has been almost wholly lost. The ultimate reason for the narrator's neglect is the fact that neither knife nor whirlwind can be dispensed with. Yet the scattering examples of knife and whirlwind in eastern tradition [1] bear valued testimony to the former presence of both incidents in the normal form.

He has been invited to eat. [2]

Although the evidence is scanty, it is perhaps sufficient. The trait is acceptable as the most logical method of introducing the recognition of the knife into the story. Four versions [3] say that the farmer is compelled to eat; but this is less well attested and less plausible. The insufficiency of evidence is scarcely a reason for rejecting this variation, but its lack of plausibility, i.e., the Lapp would reasonably be pictured as inviting a stranger to eat rather than as compelling a recognized enemy to do so, is ample justification for its exclusion.

His knife, he learns, had struck the Lapp's thigh. [4]

In a few versions [5] a woman (the Lapp's daughter, an unnamed woman, the mistress of the house, or a witch) is

---

The attack, which is being made at a distance, is unsuccessful. Cf. "The Leech of Folkestone," in R. H. Barham, *Ingoldsby Legends*. The tub, which should be used for the return journey, has, like the knife, been put to an entirely new use. — [1] The knife alone occurs in e 1 and f 9; both motifs occur in g 2; j 12; l 2. — [2] b 5, 10, 11; d 2; k 1, 2. — [3] a 7, 8; b 1; d 5. — [4] a 1 (actors reversed), 3—6, 8, 9; b 2 (Lapp's uncle), 3, 5, 6 (bird's wing), 8—10, 13; c 1; d 2, 6; f 9; k 1—3, 5, 6 (Lapp lies sick in bed with a wound in his thigh). — [5] a 5, 8, 9; b 9; d 2.

injured; but such meaningless and unnecessary doubling of the actors cannot be original.[1] Such versions exhibit a contamination with those tales of a witch (not a wizard) riding in a whirlwind, and the form which mentioned a woman was for some reason more familiar to the narrator. Elsewhere the trait is still more disordered: the farmer recognizes his knife sticking in a leg (i.e. thigh) of venison[2] or of beef,[3] or the injury is transferred to the farmer.[4]

Since it is Christmas eve the farmer wants to go home for the holiday.[5]

Although Christmas is supported by abundant testimony, another holiday, Kekri or All Saints' Day, which is in Finland a more ancient festival than Christmas, is frequently mentioned.[6] Kekri is meant by the "saint's day" for which lamb-stew is prepared.[7] A third holiday, Easter, has obtained a footing only in the extreme east of Finland, where Greek Catholic influence is dominant.[8] One version fixes the time as the farmer's name-day.[9] Certain versions are obscure or defective: one names a "holiday for which pies — an important part of any east Finnish festival — are prepared"[10] and those in which the day is not named as other than a "holiday".[11]

---

[1] See Aarne *Leitfaden* (FF Comm. 13), pp. 27—28; K. Krohn, *Die folkloristische Arbeitsmethode*, p. 67. — [2] b 6; k 2. — [3] b 10. — [4] b 13; k 3. — [5] a 5, 6, 9; b 2—8, 11, 12; d 2, 4; e 1, 3, 5, 9; f 5, 8—10; g 5, 7, 8; i 1; j 4; k 7; l 4, 6, 7, 11; s 1; FS; E 1. A curious muddling of the incident (k 7) relates that the traveler wishes he were at home to see what would be served for dinner on Christmas eve. The Lapp does not take him home, but promises to bring a sample of everything while the farmer bathes (cf. a 6). As further proof he engages to fetch a stocking belonging to the man's wife. Here is evidently a contamination with some other story of magical transport; cf. e 1; j 6; m 1. — [6] e 8; f 1, 3; g 2, 3, 6; j 1, 2, 6—8, 10, 11, 15; l 1, 8; m 1—6. — [7] g 1. — [8] i 4, 5. — [9] j 5. — [10] i 2. — [11] k 2, 4, 5.

In view of the distribution and numbers of the scattering variations we may reject the holiday they name, i.e., name-day, holiday for which pies are prepared, and a "holiday", and limit our attention to Christmas, Kekri, and Easter. The rejection of Easter, known only in Karelia, is obviously demanded. Between Christmas and Kekri we shall not hesitate long, the decision must favor Christmas. Christmas is widely known, both in east and west Finland. It is established in west Finland where Kekri is wholly unknown. Regarded merely as a hypothetical question, it is possible to imagine either one of these two conspicuous Finnish holidays as a substitute for the other, but their distribution takes the question out of the realm of guesswork. The holiday restricted to the narrower area is the newcomer, unless there is reason for thinking otherwise. Kekri could have given rise to Christmas, but if it had done so, then some scattering examples of Kekri would be expected in the west. The substitution could scarcely have been complete. The conclusion is then inescapable that Christmas yielded in eastern Finland to Kekri. The substitution of Kekri is due to an archaising tendency, a tendency which is quite in keeping with the culture of eastern Finland. The establishment of this fact confirms again the deduction that the tale passed from western to eastern Finland and makes possible a second deduction, that the tale spread in Finland after the conversion to Christianity.

There remain to be examined those versions in which the day of return is not mentioned.[1] These are sufficiently numerous and sufficiently widely distributed to give us pause. Of course some instances can be rejected

---

[1] a 1—3, 7, 8; b 1, 9, 10; c 1; d 1, 3, 5, 6; e 2, 4, 6, 7; f 2, 4, 6, 7, 9; g 4; i 3; j 3, 9, 12—14; k 1, 3, 6; l 2, 3, 5, 9, 10, 12.

as possessing no evidential value.[1] Yet many others[2] can scarcely have omitted this trait, had it been familiar. Consequently it is possible that Christmas itself has entered the story in place of an unnamed day. The frequency of versions in west Finland which do not name the day increases the probability of this explanation, but certainty in the matter is not to be attained. Either association with a particular holiday or the omission of the naming of the holiday is, in the circumstances, so readily accounted for that a decision cannot be insisted upon.

He is asked to give an ox in payment for the trip home.[3]

Well established as the ox is in the story, there are nevertheless competing animals, the bull[4] and the cow.[5]

Ox:

	—	2	
2	7	2	—
10	4	7	—
5			

Bull:

	5	—	
—	1	—	—
2	—	—	—
—			

Cow:

	5	3	
4	2	4	11
1	—	2	4
1			

---

[1] E.g. a 1, 3; c 1; d 3, 5; e 6, 7; f 2; g 4; j 9; l 3, 9. — [2] E.g. the carefully told narratives a 7, 8; b 1, 9, 10; f 7; k 1, 3, etc. A distinction between these and the foregoing ones of no evidential value is more or less a question of opinion, but the inclusion or exclusion of a particular version is not a matter of moment. — [3] a 2, 6—9; b 1—4, 6—9, 11, 13; 1, 2, 4, 6; e 2—3, 5—9; f 1, 4—8, 10; g 6, 7; k 5, 7; m 4, 5. — [4] b 10, 12; e 7; l 4, 6, 7, 9, 11. — [5] a 5; b 5; e 1, 4; f 3, 9; g 1, 2, 5, 8; i 1, 2, 4, 5; j 1—4, 6—8, 11, 13—15; k 1—4; l 1, 3, 5, 8, 10; m 1—3; s 1 (heifer); FS.

Among these we have accordingly to choose. The bull
may be rejected as a late introduction, a substitute for the ox,
for it is not widely distributed and is an easy development by
specialization. The choice must fall either on the ox or the
cow. The ox predominates in the west and extends well
into the east, while the cow is found only sporadically in
the west. Cultural conditions can best explain this divergence in tradition. Western Finland knows the ox, which
is used for plowing, while eastern and northern Finland
have never employed the ox to anything like as great an
extent. In other words: the story has been adapted to
new cultural surroundings and in the passage from western
to eastern Finland the ox has yielded place to the cow.
As we should expect, the replacement has not been complete
and a considerable number of instances of the ox persist
in east Finnish tradition. The very scanty number of
instances of the cow in western Finland supports this
conclusion, for it is unlikely that, if the east Finnish form
containing the cow were original, the ox would have come
even in western Finland to occupy so dominating a position.
The argument from cultural conditions is effective in one
direction but not in the reverse.

The ox is black.[1]

Variations are too infrequent, too restricted in their
distribution, and too readily explained as specializations in
one way or another to lay serious claim to inclusion in
the normal form. Thus we reject black spotted,[2] spotted,[3]
white spotted,[4] red and white,[5] and finally white.[6] Mention

---

[1] a 6, 8, 9; b 1—3, 6, 7, 11; d 1, 4, 6; e 2, 5—8, 10, 13; f 1, 3—5, 7—10; g 1, 6; i 1, 2, 4, 5; j 1 3, 4, 7, 8, 11, 13—15; k 1—3, 5, 7; l 5, 6; m 1—3; s 1. — [2] b 5; e 3; l 1, 8, 11. — [3] d 2; g 5. — [4] a 5. — [5] FS. — [6] b 4.

of the color has dropped out of several texts in which we have simply the "ox" or the "cow";[1] the "big" ox;[2] the "best" ox;[3] or the "best" cow.[4] None of these is entitled to more than passing consideration in choosing the normal trait. The adjective "black" could easily have dropped out or have been replaced by the relatively meaningless "big" or "best", while a reverse procedure, the insertion of an adjective of color, could not have led to the same result over so large an area. The evolution in one direction can be conceived, while an evolution contrariwise cannot. Black oxen are no more frequent in Finland than elsewhere and therefore it cannot be claimed that the adjective "black" was inserted in many texts because it was the usual and familiar color. Possibly an appropriateness is to be seen in associating the black ox with the Lapp, a person of ill repute, but the point cannot be insisted on. Black, i. e. Mustikki, becomes a proper name (cf. "Blackie" as a name for a cow) in a few texts,[5] but this cannot be original.

The ox is tied to the doorpost or stands in the stall nearest the door.[6]

A few texts, all eastern, put the animal in the hindmost stall;[7] but this is a recently developed tradition, scarcely consonant with the haste with which the animal is always carried off. The change stresses the difficulties overcome by the Lapp; but such emphasis has no special point in the story. The restricted area in which this modification occurs is strong confirmatory evidence of its secon-

---

[1] (Ox): a 2; b 9; m 5. (Cow): e 1, 4; g 8; j 2, 6; k 4; l 3, 10. — [2] b 4, 8; f 1; g 7; k 5. — [3] a 7; b 1. — [4] j 4; k 3. — [5] f 9; i 1, 4. — [6] a 6, 7; b 1—8, 11, 13; d 1, 2, 4, 6; e 2, 5, 8, 10; f 3—7, 9; g 6; i 2; j 3; k 1, 2, 4, 5: l 1, 5; 6, 12; m 1. "The side nearest the yard" (f 5) is evidently the side nearest the door and is included in the tabulation. — [7] g 1; j 2, 6—8, 11, 13, 15; l 3; m 2, 3.

dary nature, and we are once more reassured in putting a low value on eastern tradition. We cannot determine whether the ox stood on the right[1] or on the left[2] side, and the normal form probably did not answer the question.

Three speeds at which the return journey may be made are offered to the farmer: as fast as a black cock, a bullet, or thought, and he accepts the last.[3]

No competing form has a wide currency or any serious claim to inclusion in the normal form. The climactic arrangement rather than the anticlimactic is more nearly primitive. The variations in matters of detail confirm the choice and arrangement of speeds as given. Thus it is clear that the slowest speed is that of a black cock, which is generally reported,[4] and confirmation is afforded by the mention of a bird,[5] of a gray hen,[6] and of a crow.[7]

---

[1] d 6. — [2] b 4; f 4. — [3] a 5, 6, 8; b 6, 9—12; d 1—4, 6; e 8; f 1; k 2 (in a slightly distorted form: gray hen instead of black cock); l 8. The versions b 4, g 3, 7, have lost the first member of the triad; the versions a 7, b 7, e 1 have lost the middle member, Equivalent to these are the versions in which the speeds are named in the same terms, but in reverse order (a 9; b 3, b 8). In l 5, where the order is similarly reversed, the slowest speed has been lost, while j 14, k 3, l 12 have dropped the fastest speed after the reversal, and b 1, which is still more muddled, also shows evidence of reversal: thought, black cock, [as fast] as he came. — [4] See the references in the preceding note. — [5] g 6; i 2, 4; j 10; l 7; m 5; s 1; FS. The distribution shows that this simpler form, a generalization, cannot be original, for the insertion of a new specialized trait (such as the black cock would necessarily be) could not be the same over so large an area. This is additional evidence that the eastern stock of tradition is inferior and secondary in origin. — [6] e 1; f 7; i 1; j 4, 9, 13, 14; k 2, 3; l 4, 12. The gray hen (Tetrao tetrix) is closely related to the black cock (Tetrao urogallus). The process of associative thinking is obvious in this exchange. — [7] b 2, 5.

Accidental variations are the pickerel of j 11, on which we shall remark in a moment, and "as flax burns in a fire".[1] Inconsequential are the following variations in the second speed offered to the farmer: crow, cock, thought (b 5); cock, hen, thought (j 1); hen, pickerel, thought (j 9); pickerel, cock, thought (j 11); hen, cock, thought (i 4); bird, fish, thought (m 5).[2] The origin of the series containing the cock and the hen is obvious: the hen has been inserted as a contrast to the cock and at the expense of the original trait. The fact that the introduction of the hen destroys the climactic series is a sufficient reason for excluding it from consideration. This insertion occurred at least twice[3] and presumably independently, for the order varies. The series bird, fish, thought is clearly a generalization. The fish, usually a pickerel, of the eastern versions[4] is further evidence of the deterioration of the story in the east; the change is evidently owing to the desire to offer conveyance by earth, water, and air. An ancient trait cannot be found in the arrow of the following: cock, arrow, "here and there" (i 1); bird, arrow, thought (i 4)[5] or the wizard of the corrupt series: cock, wizard.[6] One version[7] has: bullet or lightning, thought, in which the first member has been lost and the second doubled. The series: crow, thought, cock[8] is also muddled. A few other variations in the second member have already been noted and explained. Nothing in all this, so far as it is new and different, can be original or representative. The cor-

---

[1] g 2. — [2] I omit for the sake of brevity the adjectives "black", which is always applied to the cock, and "gray", which is always applied to the hen. — [3] j 1; l 4. — [4] j 9, 11; m 5. — [5] Note that the arrow of these forms explains the journey *in* an arrow of m 1 and m 2. The arrow seems to be an archaizing substitute for the bullet; see Kaarle Krohn, *Die folkloristische Methode*, p. 77. — [6] e 5. — [7] b 4. — [8] b 2.

ruption rampant in eastern tradition need only be pointed out again; it has just been amply documented once more.

In regard to the third member, thought, there is little difficulty. Some variants have, as has been noted, reversed the order. Others replace the idea, "as fast as thought", by equivalents and paraphrases: "here and there";[1] "from here I take and there I throw" (i 2); "as fast as he wants" (g 2); "as fast as he came" (b 1). The choice between going in dreams or awake (j 8) illustrates a loss of both slower speeds. The series: crow, thought, cock (b 2) is clearly corrupt. Nothing in all this, so far as it is different, is original or representative.

The episode of the three speeds is an old one,[2] and properly associated with demons, devils, and magicians generally. Famous is its employment in the *Faustspiel*, whence Lessing took it, although it is not found in Goethe's *Faust*. So far as a cursory survey shows, the Finnish form of the episode is characteristic and individual. It is possible that the association of this episode with the figure of the Lapp is ultimately explicable by the medieval tradition which declared that Lapps sold knotted ropes to mariners. When the first knot was opened a gentle breeze sprang up, the second provided a stronger wind, and the third a hurricane.[3] But this tradition does not appear in the

---

[1] e 1; i 1; s 1. — [2] An analogue has been taken down in Sweden (*Bidrag til kännedom om de svenska landsmålen*, 1882, A II, 7, 33), but it occurs in another connection. See in general R. Köhler, "Schnell wie der Gedanke", *Euphorion*, I (1894), 47—51. To this note Professor Bolte adds in a letter of June 12, 1924 to Professor Kaarle Krohn: Jegerlehner, *Sagen aus dem Oberwallis*, 1913, p. 293 (i, 3); Zingerle, *Sagen aus Tirol*, 1891, No. 479; Jegerlehner, *Blümlisalp*, 1917, p. 125; *Zs. d. dt. Palästinavereins*, X (1887), 167; *Zs. des Vereins f. Volkskunde*, XX (1910), 82. — [3] See Feilberg, *Bidrag*, II, 228 (knude); IV 1058 (vind), 1062 (vindknude); J. R. Aspelin, "Entisestä tuulenkaupasta Suomessa", *Suomen Museo*, VIII (1905) No. 1, p. 5—7, cf. XII, No. 2, p. 46 (German

Finnish versions of the "Black Ox". We shall, however, meet it again.

Some versions do not have three speeds for the return. Those which make no mention of any speed are seen at once to be defective and meaningless.[1] Those tales in which the return is not described are either on other counts not truly representative[2] or are imperfectly recorded.[3] A number of versions imply that the return journey was made with great speed, without mention of three offered speeds. In two of these the three speeds are clearly implied: in i 5 (where the first and second devil refuse and the third carries off the farmer so fast that his hat falls) and j 5 ("Three brothers. Third the driver"). The remaining versions in which a terrific speed is described or implied without mention of the choice among three speeds are rather numerous.[4] They will be found to fall into two classes, one in which the farmer loses his hat[5] and one in which he is put to sleep on a bench before the journey begins.[6] A few which fall into neither class are clearly defective.[7] The origin of the first class is readily seen to be the omission of the episode of the choice of the three speeds, for the episode of the loss of the hat is regularly part of the story, as will be shown later. The version m 4 is a particularly clear example of such an omission. The second class is also a development out of the normal form of the story, as we shall see.

abstract in *Anzeiger der Finnisch-ugrischen Forschungen*, XIV (1914), p. 135, No. 337; Kaarle Krohn, Lappische beiträge zur germanischen mythologie, *Finn.-ugr. Forsch.* VI (1906), pp. 173—5. — [1] a 1; e 6; g 4; j 7; l 9, 11; m 6. A speed is implied but not described in some instances: e 2, 7; k 1; E 1. — [2] a 3; c 1; d 5; i 3; j 12; k 6; l 2; k 7 is confused with the Cymbeline motif; cf. e 8; j 6; m 1, 3. — [3] l 3, 9. — [4] b 13; e 2, 4, 7, 9; f 2—6, 8—10; g 1, 5, 8; j 2, 3, 6, 15; k 1, 4; l 1, 6; m 1—4; E 1. — [5] b 13; e 9; f 2, 4, 5, 8—10; g 1, 5; j 6; m 1, 3. — [6] f 3; g 8; j 2; l 1, 6; m 2. — [7] e 2, 4, 7; f 6; j 3, 15; k 1, 4.

Tales of a traveler who is carried home by a demon or the devil are frequently met with in Scandinavian countries and elsewhere. A simple Danish tale, which may be compared with f 7 or FS, will serve as an illustration:

A Danish skipper who is lying in a Norwegian harbor on Christmas day happens to remark to a restaurant-keeper (a woman) that he should like to be home for dinner. She thinks it not difficult and asks a specie dollar as pay. He goes on board and at once a fresh breeze rises and bears him home within the day.[1]

The similarities to the "Black Ox" are negligible; the fixing of the time as Christmas and the payment for the journey are more or less implied by the theme itself. More significant is such a tale as the following, which represents the materials out of which the "Black Ox" was formed:

A man from Salling is sauntering about in Copenhagen in ill humor because it is Christmas and he cannot get home. A stranger engages him in conversation and learns of the difficulty. The stranger, a demon (bjærgmand) of Jutland, thinks that it can be easily overcome and volunteers to take him home for a future unnamed service. They fly through the air on horseback and when they have been riding an hour, the horse bearing the man stumbles. "That was the tower of Viborg church", explains the demon. The demon says on reaching the man's house that his services will be wanted in a few days to ferry the departing elves across the sound, and so it turns out.[2]

---

[1] E. T. Kristensen, *Danske Sagn,* I, 417, No. 1338. On the subject of such rapid conveyance see in general Feilberg, *Bidrag,* II, 457 (luftrejse). — [2] Kristensen, *Danske Sagn,* I, 411—12, No. 1330. All the tales from No. 1329 to No. 1338 are similar in theme. The last incident in the present tale is familiar to every reader as the "Ueberfahrt der Zwerge"; see Grimm, *Deutsche Mythologie*[4], pp. 693—4, III, 248; Taylor, "Northern Parallels to the Death of Pan", *Washington University Studies,* X (1922), 45, n. 76.

These speeds are suggested by the Lapp.[1]

The wide distribution of this form speaks strongly in its favor. It is, furthermore, logical that no new figure should be introduced merely to suggest the speeds. There are, however, many texts in which accessory figures have been added for this purpose. Thus two eastern versions[2] in which there are but two speeds have two Lapps as the suggesters of these speeds. These versions are, according to any explanation, fragmentary. A much greater importance attaches to the large number of versions in which the three speeds are suggested by the Lapp's three sons.[3] Some variations are readily explicable. In a few texts[4] the emphasis has been shifted slightly so that the suggesters of the speeds are brothers rather than sons. In one version the sons are replaced by daughters, — a change for the sake of contrast.[5] Again the suggesters are the daughter, the son, and the wife.[6] In b 2 the uncle proposes all three speeds. Elsewhere the relationship has been forgot-

---

[1] a 7; b 3, 7, 8, 10, 11; d 3, 6; e 1; j 1; k 3, 5; l 1, 5, 12; s 1. A wizard suggests them in b 1; f 7. The texts e 3 and e 8 are obscure. Cf. b 2. — [2] e 5; g 3, 7. See also j 10 and j 13. — [3] a 5, 6; b 5, 6, 9; d 1, 2, 4; f 1; g 2, 7; j 4, 9, 11, 14; k 2; l 4; m 5. It is possible to subject these texts to a further examination regarding the order in which the sons appear. In four districts the youngest son speaks first (a 5, 6; b 6; d 2, 4; g 2) and only a little less frequently does the eldest speak first (b 5, 9; d 1; j 11). Those instances in which no comment is made on the order are chiefly current in the east, where we are by now accustomed to find less well preserved forms (f 1; j 4, 9, 14; k 2; m 5). The order in which the youngest speaks first is original, as is shown by its distribution and by its complying with Olrik's law of *Achtergewicht* (i.e., the most important person is last in the series). See further Kaarle Krohn, *Die folkloristische Methode*, p. 101. — [4] g 6; j 5; l 7, 8, 11. — [5] FS. — [6] b 12. Note also father and son in j 10 and j 13.

ten entirely so that we have three men,[1] three little men,[2] or three demons.[3] We are thus confronted with the necessity of deciding whether the speeds were suggested by the Lapp or by his three sons. Numerically the versions are about equally divided between the two forms. The geographical distribution gives no clue as to which is the original. A reason which has already been given enables us to reach a decision, viz., it is unnecessary to bring new actors into the story. The introduction of the three sons into the story took place at a relatively early period inasmuch as the enlarged form attained to such a wide distribution. It is altogether probable that the eastern texts in which the speeds are suggested by three demons or by three men represent a splitting of the figure of the Lapp as the suggester of the three speeds, a splitting which is quite independent of the motif of the three sons, although analogous to it.

The return journey is made in a Lappish sleigh, i. e., a tublike or troughlike vehicle.

The vehicle is designated as "pulkka",[4] "ahkio",[5] "kotti",[6] or "pɔhdin",[7] all of which mean much the same thing. It is also called a tub,[8] a trough,[9] a vehicle shaped like a pig's hoof,[10] a chest,[11] and a sleigh.[12] From this exhibit it follows readily enough that the original vehicle was a Lappish sleigh, a vehicle resembling a tub or a trough.

---

[1] a 8; i 1, 2. — [2] i 4. — [3] i 5 and implied in a 9 and b 4. — [4] b 7, 13. — [5] e 1. — [6] d 2. — [7] a 7. — [8] d 4; cf. f 9 and the remarks above (p. 33 note 3) on this text. — [9] a 5, 6; b 2, 3, 5, 8, 9, 12; cf. f 7 and k 4. In the last three the trough is said to have been borne by a whirlwind, but this addition would seem to be borrowed from the beginning of the story. In b 7 as in b 8 the vehicle is drawn by reindeer, but this addition is an unnecessary embellishment. — [10] e 2. — [11] e 8. — [12] i 1; k 3.

Certain modifications need but to be listed to be rejected: the farmer rides on a broom through the air;[1] on the shoulders of the Lapp's eldest son;[2] on a pole;[3] on a branch of a spruce tree;[4] on the back of a fire-horse;[5] on an old fur coat;[6] on a raft;[7] in a wizard's arrow;[8] and, with complete forgetfulness of the means, "through the air"[9] or "with his eyes covered".[10] In all these no one will see more than a hazy recollection of the original mode of travel. Furthermore, the corruption of the eastern versions is apparent.

Some tales make little or no mention of the actual means of transportation, which is accomplished by hocuspocus, expressed or implied. In such tales[11] the farmer is put to sleep (or awakes in the morning) at the table. Although scarcely any single one of these narratives is in itself sufficiently full and detailed for us to maintain with complete assurance that the episode of the transportation in a sleigh is lacking in it, their number is so large and the contradiction to such a means of conveyance so clearly implied that these tales certainly represent a different form of considerable vitality. This new form is distinctly east Finnish in its distribution; d 4 is the only western instance, and d 4 itself is not free from the suspicion of east Finnish influence, for it was taken down from a west Finnish source in Mäntyharju, i.e. in f (South Savolax), an east Finnish district. The cleft between east and west Finnish tradition gapes, and we are again forced to decide which possesses the prior form. Are there west Finnish tales which show the beginnings of a development which might

---

[1] b 11. The trait is obviously borrowed from the habits of witches. — [2] b 6. — [3] f 4; g 1; k 1. — [4] k 5. — [5] j 6. — [6] j 3. [7] j 1. — [8] m 1; see the remarks on p. 41, note 5. — [9] f 6; g 7; i 4. — [10] e 9; cf. b 13. — [11] d 4; e 5; f 1, 3, 7; g 7, 8; j 2, 10; l 1, 4, 5, 6 (sofa), 8, 12; m 1, 2. Cf. j 6, 8 (travels in a dream).

culminate in this east Finnish form or vice versa? Is the east Finnish form entirely harmonious within itself or does it display traces of internal conflicts betraying a later rise? To the latter question an answer is easily given: the east Finnish tradition is not harmonious within itself. The farmer awakes in the morning at his own table, but this event may be preceded either by the episode of the sleighride, which flatly contradicts the scene of his awaking at a table,[1] or by the farmer's lying down to sleep,[2] which is of course entirely harmonious. The remaining versions[3] are scanty in the extreme and, except for e 5, which will be taken up later, offer nothing of interest. Our interest turns on those tales in which the description of the transporting of the farmer seems to conflict with the scene of his awaking at his own table. Several of them, each in a different way, show that the western form has yielded the eastern form, probably by contamination with a tale narrating a magic transportation of the hero while he slept. Particularly important are those versions[4] in which the farmer is put to sleep at the head of the table and in which there persist characteristic details of the journey in a Lappish sleigh: in d 4; f 7; g 7, and m 1 the farmer's hat blows off — an incident which can scarcely be appropriate in the magic transportation of a man sleeping on a bench – and in l 1 the Lapp tells the farmer to lie on a bench and to move toward the end when it bumps the first time, then nearer the end, and at the third bump to drop off, when he will be at his own table. The blowing off of the farmer's hat distinctly implies the journey in a sleigh, and this fact will be still clearer in the following discussion of the incident of the loss of the hat. The true context of the bumps will be fully apparent later; they can only

---

[1] d 4; f 7; g 7; j 2; m 1; cf. j 6, 8. — [2] j 10; l 1, 4, 6; m 2. — [3] e 5; f 1, 3; g 8; l 8, 12. — [4] d 4; f 7; g 7; l 1; m 1.

be the three bumps of the sleigh against the church steeples. These versions, which are intelligible only by comparison with those containing the journey in the sleigh, afford conclusive proof of the secondary nature of the eastern stock of tradition. The texts d 1; f 1 (cf. f 3); g 7, 8 may possibly be representative of an intermediate form, for, although the farmer is transported in the usual way, they contain the special remark, "Man appears at table", and the suggestion lying behind this is presumably the farmer's desire to be home for the Christmas feast. Another clue to the course of development is seen in b 13: "Lapp puts him in sleigh, ties cloth over farmer's eyes . . ." and in e 9: "Lapp covers the farmer's eyes". Furthermore, e 5 and j 8, in which the Lapp asks whether the farmer prefers to go in his sleep or while awake, [1] mediate between eastern and western tradition. Through such intermediate forms and aided by the similarity to some tale in which the hero fell asleep to be transported across long distances the eastern stock of tales can be imagined as developing.

The speed of the return journey is that of thought. [2]

Inasmuch as this incident is a logical consequence of the original selection of the speed, a careful examination of the variations is unnecessary. The muddled versions contain nothing of consequence, and their variations [3] need not be recited in detail.

---

[1] Cf. l 12, in which the farmer hears "as in a dream" the lowing of a bull. — [2] a 2, 5, 6, 8; b 4—6, 9—12; d 1—6; f 1, 7; g 6; j 1, 4, 9—11, 13; k 2; l 4, 7, 8; m 5; (the speed of the human mind): a 7, 9; b 1, 3, 7; g 3, 7; ("here and there"): e 1; i 1, 2, 4; s 1; ("before realized"): f 4. — [3] As fast as the wind, E 1; with terrific speed, b 13; "as fast as a bullet", e 3, k 3, l 5; "a hundred times faster than a bullet", k 5; "at fast as a wizard", e 5, m 1; "so fast he wakes up at night", j 2; "as fast as a black cock", b 2, b 8, j 14, l 12; "in a wink", a 9; etc.

The farmer loses his cap, but, although he speaks when it blows off, it lies too far behind to be recovered.[1]

This may be assigned a place in the normal form, although it is possible to see that the incident has established itself in the story during the life of the story on Finnish soil. The absence of instances in a (Finland proper) and its scanty occurrence in d (South and Middle Tavastland) and k (South Österbotten) are instructive. The episode is seen in the process of establishing itself. Furthermore, it appears that the dissemination of the tale in Finland has a center in b (Satakunta), where the incident of the hat is a familiar constituent. In eastern Finland the trait acquired a new form: the farmer's hat catches on a steeple.[2] This new form may well be a reminiscence also of a trait which failed to lodge firmly in the tradition: the farmer or the vehicle bumps against a church-steeple or he strikes his foot against a cross on a church and asks the Lapp what that might be. To this the Lapp replies that it is too far back to speak of (m 4); the farmer strikes his heel against a steeple while riding in a tub (d 4); he strikes two steeples (b 4); strikes Tornio steeple and the second bump is the farmer's house (e 1); he gets out at the second bump (k 3); the trough bumps into a steeple and the farmer's cap flies off (b 8); the farmer's hat hangs on the ridge-pole of the fifth church behind him (g 7) or on an unnamed steeple (m 3); in passing Tornio his hat is brushed off by the steeple and he wakes (j 6). The bumps in l 1 are derived from this incident, although the tale has been altered in other regards. The incident of the man riding with a demon and striking churchsteeples is a familiar one in Scandinavian

---

[1] b 2, 6—8, 12, 13; d 1, 4; e 10; f 2, 4, 5, 7—10; g 1—3, 5, 7; i 1, 2, 5; j 1, 4—6, 8, 9, 13, 14; k 5; m 1, 3, 4. In s 1 the incident is anticipated. — [2] g 1, 7; j 6; m 3.

story[1] and because the incident involved a magical transportation it was readily associated with the analogous incident in the tale of the Black Ox. It is also worthy of remark that such incidents of magic transportation frequently contain an episode in which the man's companion points out scenes along the route and that this episode occurs in the tale of the Black Ox.[2]

They have passed seven churches since it fell.[3]

The tales differ considerably on this point and specify also three,[4] five,[5] six,[6] nine,[7] or thirteen[8] churches, or beyond the fifth or sixth parish.[9] Although this tabulation seems at first sight to afford no basis for reaching a conclusion, some general principles of associative thought can be invoked to aid us. A number is likely to be associated either with those near to it in counting or with those enjoying a similar traditional use. Thus, "three" may suggest "two" or "four", the adjoining numbers, or "seven", also a number of mythical significance, but "three" will be unlikely to suggest "thirteen", since the difference in value is so great. A relatively large num-

---

[1] A typical example is the following tale from Småland (Sweden): A Vedland farmer goes to Stockholm with oxen. On Christmas eve he meets a man on a large black horse who asks him to mount behind. They strike the belfry of Vedland church. He is warned not to see fire before sunrise. He goes to church Christmas morning (i. e. sees fire), falls sick, and commits suicide. See G. A. Aldén, *I Getapulien*. Another example is given above, p. 44. Abundant examples may be found in H. F. Feilberg, *Bidrag til en ordbog over jyske almuesmål*, I, 599 line 53 (Hest), II, 132 line 29 (Kirketårn) and IV, 261. The obvious similarities to the tale of the Black Ox have led to its occasional introduction into the latter tale. — [2] b 1, 3—5, 9; e 1; f 2; l 10; m 4. — [3] b 6, 12; d 1; f 5, 7—10; i 1, 2; j 2. — [4] f 4; j 8, 9, 13; k 5. — [5] b 7; g 7; m 3. — [6] i 5; j 1. — [7] b 11; e 9; g 5; j 4, 5; m 1. — [8] b 13. — [9] g 2.

ber like "seven" is more likely than a small number like "three" to be associated with "nine" or "thirteen". Of course such considerations as these are serviceable in conjunction with an understanding of the number's use in the story and a due regard for its distribution in the variants. In the tabulation before us we can discard "thirteen" for various reasons: (1) its infrequency and (2) limited distribution, as well as (3) its relative inappropriateness in the story, for "thirteen" is a larger number than is needed. But the occurrence of "thirteen" is not without value to us, since it is an indication that the original number here was, as might be expected, a number with mythical or traditional associations. The number "six" is discarded because of (1) infrequency and (2) the readiness with which it can be derived from "seven", which is both more suited to the story and more widely disseminated. When the Lapp and the farmer are in the seventh parish, the hat lies six churches behind them. Similarly, "beyond the fifth or sixth parish" is a witness for "seven".

We are thus reduced to a closer consideration of "three", "five", "seven", and "nine". The predominance of the larger numbers leads us to expect a large number as original. This is a rather strong argument against "three". Furthermore, the distribution of "three" is scanty. And finally, not all the other numbers can be readily derived from "three". Such numbers as "five", "six", "nine", and "thirteen" are not immediately suggested by "three". For these various reasons we shall reject "three" temporarily with the possibility of returning to it, *if nothing better can be found*. "Five" has little to commend it; it does not give a good explanation of the rise of the other numbers and its own appearance can be readily explained as an introduction from counting by the decimal system. We have already seen that "seven" affords an explanation for several other numbers. More than this, "seven" is widely distributed and serves a useful purpose in the story. The most important observation concerning "seven" is, however, the fact that all the other numbers can be readily derived from it. These facts and the rather wider distribution of "seven" incline us to favor it. "Nine" is not particularly attractive because it does not associate itself easily with such numbers as "five", "six", and "thirteen". The upshot of the matter is that "seven" is selected as the normal form.

An altogether natural substitution and one in the direction of modernizing the story is seen in those tales in which the distance is measured in the ordinary manner; the cap lies 400, 500 or 5 kilometers (40 penikulma,[1] 50 penikulma,[2] or five versts)[3] behind. An equally natural distortion is found in the tale f 9, in which the Lapp returns to fetch the cap, although it lies seven parishes behind.

A trait unknown elsewhere among the variants of this tale occurs frequently in Satakunta: the driver asks the farmer if he recognizes certain places on the route.[4] This invention, which is familiar in other tales of magic conveyance, has acquired a local currency; but it has not established itself in a wider area.

On his return he (or another at his command) visits the stable.[5]

Whether he goes himself or whether he sends another, as is almost as widely asserted,[6] is not easy to determine.

---

[1] b 2. — [2] b 8; g 3. — [3] g 1; j 14. — [4] b 1, 3—5, 9. See the Danish tale printed above (p. 44) and the references given there. — [5] a 6—9; b 1, 2, 6, 7, 10, 12, 13; d 2, 4, 6; e 1, 2, 5; f 7—9; g 7; j 3; l 5; m 4 (in the morning); s 1; E 1. The episode is often implied in other texts, e. g., b 3; d 1; i 1, 2, 5, etc. The tabulation is necessarily incomplete. — [6] Wife (b 5; e 9; i 4; k 2); family (a 9; b 1, 2, 6, 10; g 8; j 1); maid (b 8; k 5); servants (b 11; k 4; m 2); hired man (b 4); women of the household (i 2; m 1, 3); children (f 9).

So simple a story as this does not need an additional figure in its economy, but the widely diverging evidence does not make for certainty in the matter.

His purpose is to forestall the Lapp.

The evidence is not abundant, but is no doubt sufficient. The farmer is unwilling to surrender the promised animal;[1] he orders a poorer one substituted;[2] he orders the barn door to be locked;[3] the cow is ordered to be moved to another stall,[4] or blessed to prevent witchcraft;[5] the farmer commands the whole family to hinder the Lapp;[6] or he pretends to forget the bargain.[7] In k 1 the episode is much expanded:

The Lapp orders the black cow to be tied in the yard on three consecutive Thursdays. An ox which is tied to the post on the first Thursday is lifted into the air, but it is not carried off. The second time the cow is tied to the post with the same result. The third time the ox is tied to the post, but the whirlwind carries off the cow.

Certain tales contain accidental or whimsical variations, e. g. he invites the Lapp in,[8] but the state of mind which they presuppose is the same and was indicated in the normal form. The stability of this trait in western tradition confirms this opinion. The farmer was unwilling to surrender his ox, but it is not clear that he practised any stratagem to hinder the Lapp.

Evidence that he took no steps to make the removal of the ox difficult is probably seen in those variants in which the farmer willingly yields it up: he brings out the ox,[9] goes into the stable to let it out,[10] or asks for it.[11] Once[12] the cow is put into the vehicle in which the farmer

---

[1] f 10. — [2] b 1, 4; k 2; and in b 8 and k 5 a smaller one. — [3] a 8, 9; b 2. — [4] k 4. — [5] b 5. — [6] b 10. — [7] k 3. — [8] b 3, 4. This episode may be an echo of the Lapp's invitation of the farmer. — [9] b 7; d 6. — [10] a 6; e 2. — [11] e 1. — [12] a 5.

had come. A variation characteristic of eastern texts[1] is that in which the farmer tells his family not to regret the loss of the cow, since he had promised it for his return.[2] These various developments have arisen from a neutral form and afford evidence that the farmer made no overt act to block the Lapp.

We reject at once those versions in which the Lapp either leaves some memento of his visit or carries away more than the cow. Such supplementary details are accidental in origin, being either casual expansions of the narrative or borrowings from some other story. Thus he leaves the animal's head, and the skull is still preserved in the stable loft;[3] or he carries off the stable door,[4] a gold ring from the forefinger of the farmer's wife, or the wife's left stocking.[5]

The ox lows as it is carried off.[6]

The trait is imperfectly recorded, and a tabulation of the versions in which it is lacking will not be instructive.

---

[1] e 5; f 5; m 1, 3; cf. f 9; E 2. — [2] This incident is so clearly marked as east Finnish that we can safely say that the Estonian version (E 2) in which it appears is of east Finnish origin. — [3] m 4, 5. — [4] j 2, 11. — [5] The last two tales are j 6 and e 8 respectively. The confusion represents some sort of entanglement with the Cymbeline motif; see also m 1 and m 3. A Swedish tale (Bondeson, *Historiegubber på Dal*, pp. 165—66) suggests how this contamination may have arisen. The tale is as follows: On Christmas eve a soldier who is serving in Finland during the war wants to go home. A "Finnekona" (Finnish or Lapp woman) tells him to seat himself on a bundle of straw and warns him not to reveal himself. He passes two churches. At home he sees his wife in the company of a shoemaker and takes a shoe from each. The intent of this story is quite different from that of the "Black Ox", but the similarities are so numerous that the association of the narratives is a ready one. — [6] b 7, 8, 12, 13; d 2; e 2, 5; k 2, 3; l 12. Clearly the swinging ox-tail in g 7 and the empty chains in f 7 are reminiscences of the swinging chains in a 6.

Yet the present tabulation will lead to a conclusion which has been implied in the comments on other traits. The absence of instances of this trait in a (Finland proper), which lies in the extreme southwest, is noticed here as so often before. The tradition in Finland proper (a) belongs distinctly to the west Finnish stock, but in many minor details it seems to diverge. The tales in Satakunta (b) conform much better to the usual form of the story. Finland proper (a) here, as so often, represents an earlier, less elaborated form. For example, certain traits of the versions taken down in a, e. g., the infrequent mention of Lapland as the goal of the journey and of Christmas eve as the occasion for the return as well as the complete absence of the episode of the lost hat, are now seen in their proper light: these episodes have not yet established themselves in the story. They do so in Satakunta, and from the form thus created has arisen in the main the east Finnish stock.

By way of summary it will be convenient to have before us what has been established as the normal Finnish form of the tale. It is as follows:

A farmer who is haying throws a knife at a passing whirlwind. He sets out for Lapland. When he has arrived there and after he has been invited to eat in a Lapp's house, he sees his own knife again. His knife, he learns, had struck in the thigh the Lapp who was traveling in a whirlwind. Since it is Christmas eve the farmer wants to go home for the holiday. He is asked to give a black ox in payment for the trip. The ox is black and is tied to the doorpost or stands in the stall nearest the door of the cow-stable. Three speeds at which the return journey may be made are offered: as fast as a black cock, a bullet, or thought, and he accepts the last. These speeds are suggested by the Lapp. The return journey is made at the speed of thought. It is made in a Lapp sleigh, i. e. a tub-like or trough-like vehicle. The farmer loses his cap, but, although he speaks when it blows off, it lies too far behind to be recovered: they have already passed seven churches since it fell. On his return he at once visits the stable. His purpose is to forestall the Lapp, but the ox is gone. The ox lows as it is carried off.

The reconstructed tale is an idealized picture of Finnish tradition. Whether this particular form had actual existence is not a matter of great moment. Indeed some details must have been more fully told in any actual oral tale: the lack of motive in the farmer's throwing the knife, the exact impulsion or ailment which drove him to make the journey, the behavior of the Lapp toward the man who threw the knife, and no doubt still other matters were explained more carefully than they are in the reconstruction. A painstaking study of the available material, particularly if this available material were somewhat fuller in its details, might possibly determine such matters. But it is not important to settle them. By the process of reconstruction we have learned the most interesting thing about the tale: its history in Finland. We have discovered that the story entered Finland in the southwest and extended its influence over practically the whole of Finland, reaching far into Karelia. More than this we can scarcely expect the reconstruction to tell us. Yet it has given us some important indications regarding the prehistory of the tale: some traits have been signalized as presumably older than the usual Finnish form.

The spread of a folk-tale has been compared to successive waves[1] and the figure is illuminating. It will be more illuminating if we conceive the waves to be waves of lava which in hardening leave permanent record. Thus the tale of the Black Ox spread over Finland proper, i. e. a (Varsi-

---

[1] W. Anderson, *Kaiser und Abt* (FF Comm. 42), p. 403, n. 2.

nais-Suomi), and left behind the versions a 1—9. It flowed on over Satakunta (b), perhaps reinforced by new outpourings, and incorporated into itself new elements which united intimately with the stream. The materials with which it had fused appear in versions b 1—13, which show the evidences of new contacts. Such new contacts may alter the stream only slightly and temporarily, — as is the case, for example, with the incident of the farmer's being asked whether he recognizes various scenes on the return journey, — or more fully and permanently, — as is the case with the fusion of the three incidents already mentioned (Lapland as goal, Christmas as day of return, and the loss of the hat). On into eastern Finland where it met new conditions the tradition poured and altered as it flowed: the ox becomes a cow, the sleigh-ride becomes a magic transportation of a different kind, the farmer comforts his wife for the loss of the ox, and old constituents of the story are lost. A stemma might seem to provide a satisfactory symbol for this development, but it does not. At the same time that new forms, which may either be chance creations[1] or truly representative of the state of affairs in the traditional stock at the moment, are being created, the old tradition, perhaps more or less permanently altered by its contacts, pours on in steady flood. If in the case of the Black Ox a stock of versions from earlier centuries had been available, it might have been possible to assign dates to the successive waves in the flood of tradition, the one overtaking and perhaps overwhelming the other.

From the mention of churches and of Christmas we see that the dissemination of the tale in Finland took place after the introduction of Christianity, that is to say, its appearance and spread are relatively late. This deduction raises the question whether the tale is in its elements a

---

[1] E. g. b 3; f 9; m 2, 5, etc.

Finnish invention. The tale contains, furthermore, traits employed elsewhere: the knife thrown into the whirlwind, the choice among three speeds, the magical conveyance, and the ride in which the hero strikes against church spires. The wide familiarity with these traits in other connections and in other countries also raises doubts as to the purely Finnish character of the tale. Finally, we may recall that the passage of the tale from west Finland, where Swedish is spoken to a considerable extent and where Swedish influences have long been felt, to east Finland has been shown. These observations, which can be made now that the normal form of the Finnish tale has been obtained, lead us to look for parallels; and our eyes turn naturally to Scandinavia. All but one of the episodes in the Finnish tale are found again in Scandinavian tradition. The components of the Finnish story are, it will be recalled, as follows: 1) whirlwind; 2) knife throwing; 3) journey; 4) recognition of knife; 5) Christmas; 6) offering of three speeds; 7) "as fast as thought"; 8) magic conveyance; 9) striking church spires on the way; 10) payment of an ox. All of these various elements — except 7, "as fast as thought" — occur in Scandinavia, although the whole list is never found together. In this situation one might maintain that the highly organized Finnish type had yielded in its decay the Scandinavian variants each of which preserved part and yet not all of its source. Per contra, it would be equally reasonable in the domain of logic to assert that the Finnish normal form is a version as valid as any Scandinavian text, and concurrent with them all; that the Finnish form combines ingeniously and imaginatively into a new pattern materials offered by the Scandinavian tradition. Obviously a critical examination of the relations of the traditions on each side of the Gulf of Bothnia is necessary to solve this dilemma.

A systematic survey of the ten episodes in the Finnish tale will prove to be the easiest method of attack on the problem. This procedure is now practicable because we have gained some notion both of the stability of the various episodes and of their respective functions in the story. This procedure will not differ in principle from that employed in the detailed study of the Finnish versions, but it must be more superficial because of the scanty materials. It can risk being more superficial in its method both because our familiarity with the story and its constituent elements will save us from serious error and because the results for which we are looking are of a general sort. We are looking for the antecedents of a specific Finnish tale and are no longer trying to define the tale itself.

We shall examine the episodes in their sequence: 1) The whirlwind appeared to be firmly seated in west Finnish tradition. Its association is more or less casual because its function is to provide an explanation of the farmer's journey. The evidence of the Scandinavian versions confirms our opinion of the instability of this episode. It is found in one of the two Swedish texts and not in the Norwegian. In other words, the associating of the whirlwind with our tale had begun in Scandinavia, and perhaps specifically in Sweden. The existence of tales in which the whirlwind is absent, and in which moreover it could never have been present, supports the belief that the whirlwind has attached itself to the tale. 2) The knife throwing is intimately associated with the whirlwind and stands or falls with it. The Norwegian tale is instructive in showing another employment of the knife incident in which the whirlwind is absent. It does not seem possible to determine whether the Norwegian tale is here preserving a much altered form of the whirlwind + knife incident or not; if the knife of the Norwegian is independent of the knife in the other incident, as is entirely possible, its presence may nevertheless explain the introduction of the whirlwind + knife episode into the story. (3) The trip to Lapland, which is so characteristic of the Finnish normal form, yields information of great value. It will be remembered that some doubt existed regarding the goal of the farmer's journey. Was Lapland originally the farmer's goal? What was the significance of those versions in which he dealt with a demon rather than with a man as in the normal Finnish form? We see now that the story was originally told of a demon, perhaps a forest demon, who was later replaced by a Lapp. The process of replacement had begun sporadically in Sweden and became all but established in Finland, where only occasional reminiscences of the original story persisted. In one Swedish version the man is lost in the woods and comes to a Lapp's cabin. This is strikingly like the Norwegian in which a wood spirit takes the man home. In the second Swedish tale the journey is firmly established as a journey to Lapland, and is not a visit to a Lapp's cabin in the woods, which is nearly the same, but not just the same thing. The conversión of a story about a demon into a story about a Lapp is taking place before our eyes. It is clear that just this transformation is going on, for the same Swedish tale which mentions the journey to Lapland veers and becomes unintelligible without the aid of the Norwegian version. It relates that the man goes to Lapland for aid "against a wicked neighbor who has set a bear on his cattle". This is no usual sort of neighbor, and just what is meant by the phrase appears from the Norwegian tale in which the wood spirit has bears under his protection. The Swedish tale is consequently midway between the Finnish and the Norwegian: it has the trip to Lapland in common with the Finnish and the demon associated with bears in common with the Norwegian. And the development has been from something resembling the Norwegian tale into something resembling the Finnish tale, and not vice versa. The Swedish tale is intelligible only as a simplification and rationalization of the Norwegian; a contrary explanation is impossible. (4) The recognition of the knife is found in all three countries, and the Finnish and Swedish versions are most nearly related. The relation of this episode to the episode of the whirlwind has already been discussed. (5) Christmas as the day of return is found in the Norwegian and one Swedish text. No particular consequence attaches to this trait as an indication of relationship, since the intent of the story might at any moment cause the introduction of a holiday, and therefore of course notably Christmas, as the occasion of the return. On the other hand some importance may attach to the fact that one Swedish version and the versions found in Finland proper (a) make mention of no day. (6) The offering of three speeds is well established in Finnish tradition, and appears in a form which seems to be related to other narratives. So far as we can see, its introduction into the story is a purely Finnish development. Yet we may perhaps see the suggestion for its introduction in the Swedish episode of the rope with three knots. All mention of three speeds is absent in the Norwegian and in many east Finnish versions, and we may conjecture in view of the similarity to other widely distributed narratives of a magical conveyance in which a single speed regularly appears and in view of the needless complication which this episode brings with it that the oldest form of the story had but a single speed. If this conjecture is correct, it follows that the east Finnish versions were carried thither before the episode of the speeds had established itself so firmly in the tale. (7) The selection of a speed as fast as thought is solely Finnish. No hint of it is found in Scandinavia, so far as the "Black Ox" is concerned. (8) The magic conveyance is the core of the tale and is of course found in Scandinavia as well as in Finland. One Swedish version has even the Lappish sleigh of the Finnish normal form. The second Swedish version, which in other regards is closely related to the Norwegian version, has the farmer sit on a stump, which, one conjectures, is connected in some way with the stump in the Norwegian tale on which the hunter lays his knife. In the Norwegian the man rides on the sleigh runners, an act which may possibly be related to the journey in the Lappish sleigh. Swedish tradition occupies clearly enough an intermediate position between Norwegian and Finnish tradition. (9) The traveler who strikes church spires on the return journey is seen to be getting a foothold in Finnish tradition. So far as the evidence goes, he has not entered the story elsewhere. (10) The payment for the return journey is found in the Norwegian and in one Swedish version. In the Norwegian it is a pig and in the Swedish a cow. The greater similarity of the Swedish to the Finnish is obvious, but again the Swedish occupies an intermediate position, for the whole story is entangled with the bear which is so important in the Norwegian. The second Swedish version has been deflected from its proper course by its involvement with the story of the rope with three knots. As so frequently occurs in that story, the opening of the third knot brings disaster. Although the first Swedish version also has elements from the story of the three knots, it has escaped derailment.

In summarizing the situation we see that the Norwegian and Swedish variants contain the characteristic elements of the Finnish normal form — except of course for the one completely lacking trait, "as fast as thought". Yet Swedish tradition is dependent on the Norwegian tale. The Norwegian tale could not have developed out of any Swedish text we have. Ultimately the story is of Scandinavian origin; a closer localization is impossible with such scanty evidence, although indications favor Norway. From Sweden it was borne to Finland, where it attained a characteristic, highly elaborated form, and in Finland it passed from west to east. We see moreover the manner in which the tale established itself in Finnish tradition. It was brought to Finland more than once before it received the "imprimatur". Thus a 3, for example, is no longer to be considered a corrupt and defective form, but rather an example of a related tale which has given much to the Black Ox. So also the tradition in a (Finland proper), which omits, except for a 2, all mention of Lapland, is not inferior in worth, — actually it preserves an older form of the tale. In similar fashion the table which changes into a stump with a snout (a 8) seems, like the post of k 1, to keep a last reminiscence of the stump which has various functions in the Scandinavian versions. Another wave of tradition brought to Finland most of the elements of the Black Ox in combination with the episode of the recognition of scenes along the route.[1] The wave left traces in Satakunta (b), but nowhere else. The episode in which the scenes en route are pointed out must be regarded as a competitor of the more favored incident, that in which the farmer's hat is blown off. Had both incidents found permanent lodgment in the tale, it would have been overburdened. Since the incident of the hat more effectively characterizes the flight, it received the stamp of approval. In a similar manner one can observe waves in the spread of the story: the loss of the introductory episode, the replacement of the ox by the cow, of Christmas by Kekri as well as the insertion of episodes which leave only chance traces[2] are all signposts along the path.

---

[1] It is of course possible that the combination was effected in Finland and Sweden independently; but we need not argue the matter in view of the insufficient evidence. — [2] E.g. the ring in j 6, m 1, 3 (cf. the stocking of e 8 and the knife of e 1) or the hint of the theme of Jephtha's daughter in s 1 or the curious contamination in f 9.

Some observations on the value of the further collection of folktales follow as a matter of course from such a study as this. The searching analysis of the theme is made possible only by the huge mass of Finnish variants. Without them we should be unable to determine the essential elements of the theme and to eliminate from further consideration the accidental omissions and embellishments of the respective narrators. A comparable mass of materials may fairly be said to exist in the printed and manuscript collections of Europe and the Near East to which Bolte, Polivka, Crane, Cosquin, Chauvin, and Basset have rendered access easy by their comparative studies. Any addition to this body of material is welcome and serves a useful purpose. From such countries as Spain and Greece where two cultures, the Western and the Eastern, have met such an addition will be unusually helpful. A similar importance attaches to tales from Turkey, Persia, and above all, India. A representative collection of Hindu tales from non-literary sources would enable scholars to pursue with good chance of success many a problem now beyond their powers. Yet the purpose of this study will only be fully attained, if it makes clear to the reader the importance of the slightest addition to our stock. One version, in this instance from Norway, proves to be of fundamental importance in fixing the origin and spread of the Black Ox. Without it the investigator would be handicapped, perhaps even defeated. A single tale, a single new variant can well prove as useful in another connection. The whole problem of India's share in the store of popular European narrative awaits clarification. In its solution, which can only be provided by critical study of individual themes and not by generalizing theories, any contribution from India can aid materially.

Abstracts of variants.

a (Finland proper).

a 1. V. Kallio 162 Uskela. — Finnish laborer goes to Lapland, wooes Lapp's daughter, leaves her, comes home. Revengeful Lapp throws knife into laborer's thigh. Laborer returns to Lapland to get out knife; marries girl. Lapp takes out knife. Laborer comes home with wife.

a 2. J. Numminen 62 Uusikirkko. — Farmer of Äöhö throws knife into hay-pile when whirlwind lifts it. Äöhö, troubled by deed, follows hay-pile to Lapland; is unable to return. Promises ox for return as quick as thought.[1]

a 3 (=a 4). V. Saariluoma 108, 429, Muurla. — Man eating in meadow throws knife into whirlwind, knife disappears. A few years later traveler displays knife and tells him not to throw it again into a man's thigh. He was a wizard, traveling in whirlwind.

a 5. E. Saarimaa 45 Mynämäki. — Farmer of Äöhö is threshing. While he is cutting his nails a whirlwind passes. Throws knife and swears. He is carried off by whirlwind, arriving in Lapland Christmas eve. Is anxious to go home. Youngest of three sons of wizard will take him as fast as black cock, the second as a bullet, the eldest

---

[1] Compare with this such a tale as the following: The mowers lying at rest at midday see something gray in the air which seizes a hay-pile and moves off. A maid recognizes the "Heudrachen" and begins to curse. The hay falls to the ground. While the laborers are asleep on the following day, a man comes to the maid, shakes her hand violently, and says, "Will you continue to curse me?" The maid awakes, crosses herself, and is left in peace. See L. von Schroeder, *Sitz. ber. phil.-hist. Kl.,* Vienna, CLIII (1906), no. 1, p. 32, n. 1, citing Auning, "Ueber den lettischen Drachenmythus (Puhkis)," *Magazin d. lettisch-literarischen Ges.* XIX (Mitau, 1891) no. 1, pp. 18—19.

as the human mind. Payment is white spotted cow. Man steps in troughlike vehicle and immediately finds himself in own yard. Cow is put in vehicle and disappears. — While eating at wizard's house man saw his own knife on plate. Was reprimanded for throwing knife into wizard's daughter's thigh. It wounded her when he swore. In traveling through air boots dry on his feet and split when taken off.

a 6. E. Saarimaa 58 Mynämäki. — Farmer sowing barley throws knife at violent whirlwind and swears. Feels at once urgent desire to journey; wanders aimlessly till Christmas eve. Arrives at farmhouse where he is given food, knife, and plate. Is reprimanded for throwing knife at thigh of master who was gathering seed-barley in whirlwind. Offer to take him home for black ox near the door. Three sons: youngest with speed of black cock, second with speed of bullet, eldest with speed of human mind. Sits in trough before door and is in own yard. Farmer goes to let out ox, but it is gone and chains are still swinging.

a 7. E. Vihervaara 15 Pöytyä. — Farmer throws knife at whirlwind, is carried to Lapland, where he is forced to eat. He is given back his knife and told not to throw it at whirlwinds but to say a prayer. Offer to take him home for the best ox, near the door. Between speed of black cock and human mind he chooses latter. Travels in "pohdin" (tub), which strikes on the railing of bridge. Goes to stable and finds ox gone.

a 8. E. Vihervaara 133 Vahto (taken down in Pöytyä). — While farm-folk are haying whirlwind carries off hay. Man throws knife and is borne away to unknown regions where he is forced to eat. Others swear, he says grace. Table changes to stump with snout. He longs for home. One offers to take him with speed of black cock, another with speed of a bullet, and the third, which he accepts, with speed of human mind. He is forced to eat with knife he had thrown at an old woman's thigh while she was getting hay for a calf. He eats and finds himself eating at own table. Intends to lock cow-stable, but black ox is gone.

a 9. E. Vihervaara 158 Pöytyä. — Farmer puts candles on window sill Christmas morning. When he goes out to look at them, devils carry him off in thin clothes through thick forest so that clothes are torn to bits. Is kept for a year. Devils promise to take him home for a black ox. Farmer had thrown knife at whirlwind and struck their mistress. Knife is returned when he is eating. He is reprimanded. Is asked if he prefers to go like human mind bullet, or black cock. Chooses the first and is home in a wink. People are bathing for Christmas eve. He hurries them to lock stable-door, but the ox is gone.

b (Satakunta).

b 1. J. A. Klemola 27 Loimaa. — By throwing knife into whirlwind man strikes wizard's thigh. Wizard takes knife and conjures man to him. Man is forced to eat with the knife and is asked whether he recognizes it. Is asked how he wants to go home: "Like human mind, black cock, or as he came?" Payment shall be the best black ox at the doorpost. Man chooses first speed. Is taken to a churchroof and asked if he recognizes it. „No." To the roof of another church. "No." Recognizes his own farmyard. Orders a poorer ox to be substituted, but the black ox is already gone.

b 2. F. V. Hannus 1 Mouhijärvi. — In seventeenth century an angry servant was ploughing a field when a whirlwind felled the horse and carried the man into another field. Man swore, and threw a knife into whirlwind in the thought that his master had conjured it upon him. Whirlwind bore him to Breadless Lapland. He finally gets food for his work, but is discharged in the belief that he is a spy from Häme. Works at another farm, but is discharged for falling in love with farmer's daughter. Is told to eat his last meal on Christmas eve, and recognizes his own knife. He has thrown it into thigh of farmer's uncle. He repents and wishes to return. Uncle promises to take him for the black ox by the door. Three speeds: flight of crow; human thought; black cock. Chooses third. Trough for sleigh. Cap falls off but is not picked up because it is 400 km behind. He is left on doorstep. "Good-by, the ox is mine." Orders barn locked, but ox is already going off in trough. Is reconciled to old master; promises to be obedient and god-fearing.

b 3. M. Laine 2 Lavia. — Huitu, a farmer from Mouhijärvi, is sowing rye when whirlwind throws dust in his eyes. In anger he throws knife into whirlwind. His conscience drives him to look for knife in Lapland. Starts in autumn, but arrives Christmas eve. Asks for supper at a farm, where he sees knife. Lapp reprimands him for molesting travelers. Promises to take him home for black ox at the door-post. Puts him in trough and asks: "Like human mind, bullet, or black cock?" "Like human mind." "Huis," said Lapp on starting. Stopped at top of church, stone in boiling torrent, and rail of bridge. On being questioned farmer said he did not recognize these places. At home farmer invites Lapp in; but he is gone with ox.

b 4. V. J. Langén 5 Pori. — Whirlwind disarranges farmer's piles of hay. He is eating and throws knife. He has terrible pains and goes to seek knife. Arrives at demon's home for Christmas. He is asked to eat, notices his knife, and remarks on it. Demons, "Travelers must pass unmolested." Farmer's pains soothed; wants to go home. Demons, "Like bullet or lightning?" Farmer, "Neither." Demons, "Like human mind." Farmer accepts and promises white ox from left side of door. On journey feet strike two church steeples. Farmer does not recognize the churches. Invites demon in to eat. Tells hired man to move poorer ox to left side of door. Demons disappear with big ox.

b 5. K. O. Laurila 8 Kiikka. — Huisu (former master of Reinilä, a farm in Kiikka) is walking after horses at haying time. Throws knife into whirlwind, for he has heard that Lapps hunting birds travel that way. Becomes so troubled that he goes to Lapland for his knife. Arrives Christmas eve. On being asked to eat he notices his own knife, which, as he is told, has wounded his host. Is cautioned never to throw knife at whirlwind. Longs to go home. Lapp offers to take him that evening for the black-spotted cow at doorpost. Eldest son: like a crow; second son, like black cock; youngest son, like thought. Last accepted. Is placed in trough which starts when he says. "Huis," from which he receives name. Stops three times: roof of Karkku church, Vammaskoski bridge at Tyrvää, and at home. Is asked if he recognizes these places. Tells mistress to bless cow so that wizard cannot take it, but cow is gone.

b 6. J. V. Lehto 3 Jämijärvi. — Fishermen eating on shore throw fishbones away and birds gather. Angry man throws knife into wing of one bird, which flies off. Conscience-stricken man looks for knife. Arrives in Lapland Christmas eve. Is given food. Sees knife in leg of venison and is asked if he recognizes it. Is reprimanded for cruelty to bird; Lapp was the injured bird. Man wants to go home. Lapp promises to take him for black ox from door post. Youngest, like black cock; second, bullet; eldest, human thought. Fisherman sits on shoulders of eldest son. Man's cap flies off, but is not recovered because it lies at the seventh church behind. At home man sends family to cow-stable to see what has happened. Black ox gone.

b 7. E. Salonen 3 Keuruu. — At Peltoniemi lives an industrious farmer. His boys die and his iron arms are of no avail. Goes to Lapp wiseman for counsel. On Christmas eve farmer wishes to go home. Lapp promises to take him for black ox at doorpost. Farmer is put in reindeer sleigh (pulkka), and is asked, "Like black cock or thought?" Starts; hat falls off but is not recovered for it lies five churches behind. Man goes to cow-stall to bring out ox; it bellows once, kicks, and disappears.

b 8. F. O. Viitanen 14 Mouhijärvi. — Farmer, ploughing, throws knife into whirlwind. (Had heard this causes whirlwind to disappear). Lapp, who has been wounded in leg, orders him to come after his knife or all will not be well. Farmer arrives Christmas eve. While eating he sees knife and receives it. He wants to return for holiday dinner. Lapp promises to take him for ox at door-post. Lapp, "Like thought, bullet, black cock?" "Black cock." Is put in trough pulled by reindeer. Trough bumps into steeple. Cap flies off, but is not recovered, for it lies 500 km behind. At home farmer orders maid to substitute smaller black ox. Lapp and ox in trough. Bellowing of is heard as they disappear.

b 9. Suomi, 1847, p. 60. — Old Lapp woman travels in whirlwind. Man throws knife and is forced to follow to Breadless Lapland. Man recognizes knife in woman's thigh. Offer to take him home that evening for an ox. Eldest, as fast as black cock and wind; second, as bullet; youngest, as thought. He is put in trough with youngest. Trough is set in motion by word "Huis". Stops on roof of Karkku church. This he does not recognize nor Vammaskoski bridge at Tyrvää. Third stop his own yard. Tells relatives the powerful word "Huis" and receives name "Huisu", which clings to the farm.[1]

---

[1] Cf. b 5.

b 10. Kankaanpään kansanopistolaiset 25 Mouhijärvi.
— When farmer of Koro is working in field, whirlwind raises dust. Farmer throws knife and swears. Goes to Lapland following year. Is given food, sees his knife on leg of beef. Lapp offers to take man home for black bull. Speed of black cock, bullet, or human thought. In own yard tells family to prevent Lapp. Lapp and bull gone.

b 11. V. Laurila 9 Ikaalinen. — Farmer complains of poor crops; goes to Lapland for advice. Is given food; recognizes knife he had thrown at whirlwind. Wise man tells him to catch perch with grain of barley in its mouth and sow the grain. Christmas eve. Lapp offers to take him home for black ox at door-post. Farmer surprised at Lapp's knowledge of ox. Lapp had sat in shape of kid on roof of cowstall.[1] Speeds: black cock, bullet, thought. Last chosen. Lapp and farmer sit on broom. Hat flies off but is not recovered for it lies nine churches behind. Farmer arrives in time for holiday bath. Tells servants to look for ox. It is gone. In spring farmer catches perch with barley grain, sows it, and has better harvest.

b 12. Vivi Nyberg 30 Hämeenkyrö. — Farmer learns Lapps travel in whirlwind. Throws knife at one. Goes to Lapland to seek knife. Finds it. Christmas eve. Promises best bull to be taken home. Lapp's daughter, "Like flight of black cock"; son, "Like bullet"; wife, "Like human mind." Man is put in trough and taken home in whirlwind. Cap lost, too late to pick it up, for it lies seven churches behind. At home hears bull bellow; goes to see; bull gone.

b 13. J. Tamminen 1 Ylöjärvi. — Farm folk haying; farmer at spring making birchbark dipper. Whirlwind scatters hay and carries off dipper. Farmer throws knife and swears. Whirlwind goes north. Farmer suffers apparently incurable pain in thigh. Witch advises journey to

[1] Cf. E. T. Kristensen, *Danske Sagn*, II, 140, No. 150.

Lapland whence pain had come. Farmer asks Lapps for aid and is sent further on. Enters hut where family is eating; recognizes knife. Lapp tells how knife had entered his thigh. Farmer apologizes and is cured on receiving silver buckle and brass trimmed sheath. Christmas eve. Farmer desires to return. Black ox promised. Lapp puts him in sleigh (pulkka), ties cloth over farmer's eyes, and sits in front. Through air with terrific speed. Cap left thirteen churches behind. At almost same moment pulkka descends. Farmer rises, tears off bandage. Lapp gone, bellowing of ox audible. Farmer runs to stable, ox gone.

c (Nyland).

c 1. V. Nyberg & Y. Ylänne 21 Sammatti. — Man throws knife at whirlwind. It enters Lapp's thigh. Lapp says, "Don't do that again."

d (South and Middle Tavastland).

d 1. Lilli Lilius 604 Hartola. — Man vists sages in Lapland. Is gone six weeks. Wishes he were home for good meal. Lapp will take him for black ox from door post. Eldest son, like black cock; second, like bullet; youngest, like thought. Man's hat falls, but it lies seven churches behind and is not recovered. Man appears at table, .ox gone.

d 2. Lilli Lilius 605 Längelmäki. — Old man and woman in hayfield. Whirlwind scatters hay. Man throws knife. It disappears. Conscience-stricken, he goes to Lapland. Is asked to eat, and sees knife on table. Had thrown it into thigh of Lapp woman, who was collecting hay for calf. Desires to be home for Christmas supper. Lapp will take him for spotted ox at door post. Puts man in reindeer kotti (sleigh) and advises him to drop out at third bump. Youngest son, like black cock; second, like bullet; third, like thought. Third bump is home. Ox bellows; he goes to look. Ox gone.

d 3. W. Wallin S. M. Y. A. XIV p. 183 Nastola. — Lapp brings man home from Lapland to Nastola church. First intent is to take him as fast as black cock, then as bullet, and lastly as thought.

d 4. A. H. Rakolainen 15 Hartola (taken down in Mäntyharju). — Farmer visits Lapp sages. Christmas eve. Wishes to be home. Lapp offers to take him for black ox at door-post. Youngest son, as black cock; second, as bullet; eldest, thought. Eldest chosen, tub for vehicle. Bootheel strikes cross on steeple and falls off. Lies three churches behind. Wakes up at home on bench. To see ox: it is gone.

d 5. M. Mattila 11 Tammela. — Famous wizard at Tammela who could make himself invisible steals hay from neighbor's meadow in whirlwind. Man throws knife at whirlwind. Later he works for wizard. Is made to eat butter with his own knife. Recognizes it.

d 6. E. Vihervaara 160 Tammela. — After throwing knife into whirlwind man has bad luck: cattle die. Goes to Lapland for advice. Sees own knife, which has wounded Lapp in leg, at supper in Lapp dwelling. For his advice Lapp demands black ox at right of door. Asked if he wants to return as fast as black cock, bullet, or human mind. Hardly has time to say human mind when he is at home. Goes into stall; brings out black ox; it disappears.

e (North Tavastland).

e 1. Lilli Lilius 75 Saarijärvi. — Three generations back the master of Alapiha, at Hyytiälä, goes to Lapland because of unsuccessful life. Promises cow for the trip home for Christmas. Speeds: as gray hen; second, "I am here and there." Lapp steps out and returns with knife belonging to Hyytiäinen's wife to convince farmer. They sit on Lappish sleigh (ahkio). Driver advises him to step out at second bump. First bump proves to be Tornio steeple. At home asks for cow for driver; cow is gone.

d 2. K. Krohn 124 Karstula. — Man from Pihtipudas parish goes to Lapland. On finishing his business Lapp will take him home that evening for black ox in stall next the door. Drops man in own dung-yard. Man lets out ox. It lows when carried off.

e 3. K. Krohn 4299 Karstula. — Kuoppalainen (now dead) to Lapland. Christmas eve. Black-spotted ox. Like black cock or bullet. Goes like bullet.

e 4. K. Krohn 3678 Kivijärvi. — Grandfather Hakkarainen from Kinnula village comes back from Lapland swiftly one night. Cow gone from stall.

e 5. K. Krohn 3708. Kivijärvi. — All grandfather's cattle die except black ox in stall by door and one horse. Is advised in dream to go on long journey to win luck with cattle. Goes to Lapland. Lapp gives advice and book of notes for home use. Christmas eve. Wants to go home. For black ox from doorpost Lapp promises to make him fly like black cock. Another Lapp offers speed of wizard. Accepts second. Lapp asks if he should be asleep or awake. Grandfather says his head is not strong enough for speed. Awakes at home. Asks women to see ox. On opening door it bellows and vanishes.

e 6. K. Krohn 16926 Viitasaari. — To Lapland. Black ox.

e 7. K. Krohn 16012 Pihtipudas. — Old man in Reisjärvi parsh had been to Lapland twice. Third time wizards say, "If you will let out your black bull".

e 8. K. Krohn 15335 Keitele. — Kekri eve in Lapland. Black ox from stall by door. Speeds: black cock, bullet, thought. Put in chest. Wife's left stocking disappears from top of fireplace.

e 9. E. Cederberg 3 Viitasaari. — Farmer's calves, pigs, and lambs die at birth. No remedy for great loss. Goes to Lapland for advice. Christmas eve. Lapp does magic tricks and says situation is remedied. Farmer wishes to be home Christmas morning. Lapp will take him home for black ox by stable door. Farmer assents. Lapp covers his eyes. Man feels himself flying. Hat falls off. He speaks too late, for it lies nine churches behind. In morning at home he tells wife to look in cowbarn. Ox gone. As Lapp had promised, his animals no longer die "without iron implement."

f (South Savolax).

f 1 A. Kolehmainen 5 Joroinen. — Man in Lapland wants to go home at Keksi. Lapp will take him for large ox. Sons offer speeds: as fast as black cock, as bullet, as thought. Next morning man is at head of his table. Ox is gone.

f 2. A. Kinnunen 64 Joroinen. — Pulliainen had been to Lapland. When he was taken home his hat flew off. It was not recovered, for it was lost at Kannus church and the man was in his own yard.

f 3. A. Kinnunen 34 Joroinen. — Putkonen of Pieksämäki parish goes to Lapland "to gods for cure". Kekri eve. Wishes to go home. Lapp will take him for black cow at stall door. In morning finds himself at home on bench at head of table. Cow gone.

f 4. A. Kemppi 3 Lapvesi. — Farmer's cattle die. Goes for aid to conjurers in Lapland. Conjurer will take him home for black ox from left side of stable. They sit on pole. Cap drops, but is not picked up since it lies three churches behind. Home before he realizes it. Ox gone from cowstable.

f 5. A. Kytö 8 Mäntyharju. — Man visits Lapp wiseman. Christmas eve. Desires to go home. Lapp will take him for black ox from side of cowstable towards yard. Is put in trough. Hat falls off. They have passed seventh church since it fell. Lapp takes ox. Farmer comforts family.

f 6. V. J. Tarkiainen 3 Juva. — Blomberg's cattle, being bewitched, are dying. Goes to Lapp wisemen for advice and to learn witchcraft. Returns through air a fullfledged sorcerer. Lapp carries off young ox at door-post.

f 7. V. J. Tarkiainen (Kotiseutu 1916 p. 60) Juva. — When large sum of money is stolen from farmer he goes to Lapp wisemen for advice. Learns the thief and how to recover money. Wishes to go home. Wiseman offers speed of gray hen, bullet, thought. Chooses third and promises black ox chained to door-post. Wiseman blows up strong wind which carries farmer. Hat falls, but it lies seven churches behind. Farmer awakes in morning on rear bench at home. Goes to cow-stall. Chains are empty. Regains money.

f 8. Savokarjalainen Osakunta 98 Puumala. — Man at St. Petersburg Christmas eve wishes to go home. Devil offers to take him for black ox. Hat falls off; it lies seven churches behind. Goes to cow-stable; ox gone.

f 9. Lilli Lilius 748 Kerimäki. — Finn goes to Lapland for health. Lapp shows knife which Finn lost previous summer while plowing. Lapp says he took knife while in whirlwind. Lapp brings in tub and tells Finn to stick the woman in the ribs with the knife when she appears in the water. She has caused the illness. Man cannot do it and is cured in another way. Christmas eve. Lapp will take him home for his best black cow from doorpost. Man's hat falls off; it is recovered although it lies seven parishes behind. Man tells children to look in cow-stall. Children return in tears. Cow gone.

f 10. Signe Sirén 36 Sääminki. — Man from Koitsanlahti in Parikkala parish goes to parish in northern Lapland for health. Christmas eve. Wants to go home. Wizard will take him for black ox. Hat flies off; too late, it lies seven churches behind. Is unwilling to give ox; but it is gone in morning.

g *(North Savolaks).*

g 1. Lilli Lilius 293 Tuusniemi. — Man suffering from epilepsy goes to Lapland for health. Saint's day. Wants to be home for lamb-stew. Lapp will take him for hindmost black cow. Both sit on pole of mountain-ash. Cross on church pulls off man's hat. It lies 5 km behind. Cow disappears.

g 2. K. Krohn 11033 Nilsiä. — Whirlwind disturbs man burning stumps. He throws knife at it and becomes ill. Goes to Lapland and finds man at whom he threw knife. Lapp shows knife and cures sufferer. Kekri eve approaches. Lapp calls sons. Youngest: speed of flax burning in fire; second, of black cock; third, as fast as wanted. Hat lost; it lies five or six churches behind.

g 3. K. Krohn 13861 Rutakko. — Man goes to Lapland for knowledge. Kekri eve. Black cow. Lapp's son goes in fire and can go like bullet. Another can go like thought. Man promises cow. Hat falls off; lies 500 km behind.

g 4. K. Krohn 1447 Rutakko. — Mikko Lemeinen at Tuorila village had been to Lapland.

g 5. K. Krohn 14752 Kiuruvesi. — Man with falling disease goes to see Lapp sages. Christmas eve. Colored cow from stall. Hat off. Have passed ninth church.

g 6. K. Krohn 15008 Kiuruvesi. — Karanka-Imma had been to Lapland to learn witchcraft. Was there Kekri eve. Three brothers: "As a bird"; "Bullet"; "Thought". Black ox at stall-door.

g 7. J. T. Hoffrén Nilsiä. — Farmer goes to Lapland. Christmas eve. Anxious to go home. Sorcerer will take him for large ox. Two sons: first, as bullet; second, as human mind. Second son takes farmer home. Hat off; left on ridge of fifth church back. Farmer finds himself sitting on bench at home. Goes immediately to stable. Ox's tail swings when it is carried off.

g 8. S. Paulaharju 433 Kuopio. — Man from Kuopio had been to Lapland to be cured. Homesick on Christmas eve. Lapp will take him home at once for a cow. Agrees, and awakes in morning on bench at home. "Go, look in cowbarn." One cow gone.

i (East Karelia).

i 1. O. A. Forsström, Kuvia Raja-Karjalasta p. 81 Sortavala. — Manninen at Rautalahti goes to sages' school in Lapland. Stays three years. Homesick on Christmas eve. Calls Lapp drivers and promises best cow, Mustikki (i.e., Blackie), for trip home. Three offers: like gray hen, arrow, "here and there". Third chosen. Manninen sits in sleigh. Hat off, lies seven churches back. Arrives for feast. Goes in morning to cowbarn; Mustikki is gone.

i 2. K. Krohn 7371 Suistamo. — Shemeikka visits Lapp wisemen. Pies are prepared at home for approaching holiday. Shemeikka anxious to go home, Lapps will take him for black cow at door-post. Drivers are summoned: first, as fast as bird; second, as bullet; third, "from here I take and here I throw". Third chosen. Hat lost; lies in seventh parish back. Tells women to look at cattle. Cow gone.

i 3. Virittäjä II, p. 123—24 Suistamo. — Two Shemeikkas from Repola parish lived in same house. One killed other's son. In belief that the child was lost the father goes to Fire-Lapland for advice. Takes white cloth to pay Lapp. Lapp acompanies him to woods. Collects wood for bonfire, kindles it, and jumps into bonfire. Lapp jumps out of burning coals. Appears holding a lower jaw with long beard hanging from it; recognizes it as his brother's. Lapp says uncle killed boy and buried corpse near house (where it was found later). On return saw brother without beard. Speaks to him and he disappears as Lapp has predicted.[1]

i 4. Virittäjä II, p. 125 Suistamo. — Easter eve old man Hoskonen in Fire Lapland wishes to go home. Lapp will take him for the best cow. Lapp whistles; three little men appear. Speeds: first, as bird; second, as arrow; third, as thought. In morning wife goes to stable; black cow lies dead. Lapp does not want it alive.

i 5. A. Valve 33. — Man goes to famous sages in Fire Lapland. Stays a long time and learns much. Before Easter he calls the devil and asks to be taken home. First and second devil refuse because it is Easter. Third wishes black cow. Assents. They go so fast that hat falls off; lies six parishes back. Arrives home same evening. Cow gone.

j (North Karelia).

j 1. A. Rytkönen 192 Kiihtelysvaara. — Karvinen, who was struck by an evil spirit, had been to Lapland for cure. Stays a year. Kekri eve. Wishes to be home. Lapp will take him for black cow. Puts him on raft. Speeds: gray hen, black cock, and thought. Third chosen. Hat falls off; lies six churches back. Kekri morning sends family to see black cow; cow gone.

j 2. H. Turunen 2 Nurmes. — Farmer flogged by evil spirit because of theft goes to Lapland for cure. Kekri eve. Wakes up at night at head of own table. Cow gone and door of cow-barn.

---

[1] I cannot believe that this text has anything to do with the "Black Ox", but its omission now would cause inconvenience.

j 3. J. E. Relander 19 Tohmajärvi. — Man seeks Lapp wiseman who will secretly kill his neighbor. Neighbor learns of plan, and goes also to Lapland for aid. Lapp will save his life for black cow at doorpost. Lapp brings in tub filled with water and tells man to plunge in at command. Man plunges. Bullet passes through tub along surface of water without harming man. Lapp orders man to stand on old fur coat. Thereupon he is at home. Goes to cow house; black cow gone.

j 4. K. Krohn 6962 Ilomantsi. — Farmer goes to Lapland. Christmas eve. Best cow. Three sons offer: speed of gray hen, bullet, or thought. Hat falls off, but they have passed ninth church. Man is thrown in yard, cow is gone.

j 5. K. Krohn 8530 Eno. — Man is very far from home on his name-day. Three brothers. Third the driver. Hat falls off, and lies nine churches and twelve chapels behind.

j 6. K. Krohn 8807 Lieksa. — Man at Louhi loses cattle. Goes to Lapland. Kekri eve. Demand cow from hindmost stall. Man lies on bench with all his luggage. Lapp puts him on back of fire-horse. In crossing Tornio, his hat is brushed off by steeple. He wakes. "Must not yawn any more." Cow and gold ring on wife's forefinger disappear. He is bald because hair came off when hat fell off.

j 7. K. Krohn 9646 a Nurmes. — Man on journey. Kekri near. Devil says that if he gives cow from hindmost stall.

j 8. K. Krohn 9796 a Nurmes. — Finn spends three years in Lapland to learn witchcraft. Kekri morning. Black cow from hindmost stall. Lapp asks if he wants to go in dreams or awake. Answers, "in dreams". Hat falls off; have passed third church since it fell.

j 9. K. Krohn 9796 b Nurmes. — Reijonen of Joensuu goes to Lapland. First son: as fast as gray hen;

second, as pickerel swims; third, as thought. Hat off; they have passed third church.

j 10. K. Krohn 9970 Nurmes. — Man in Lapland. Kekri. Son: as with wings of birds. Father: as thought. Birch-leaf broom for pillow.

j 11. K. Krohn 10160 Nurmes. — Trip to Lapland. Kekri. Black cow from hindmost stall. Eldest son, as a pickerel swims; second, as a black cock flies; youngest, as thought. Cow and barn-door gone.

j 12. K. Krohn 9647 Rautavaara. — Lapp travels in whirlwind. Man strikes it with knife. Falls sick and goes to Lapland for cure. Visits man he had struck. Lapp asks why he threw knife. Says it was cause of illness. Lapp returns knife. He recovers.

j 13. K. Krohn 11148 Rautavaara. — Man from Lieksa parish goes to Lapland. Hindmost black cow. Father, like gray hen; son, like thought. Son is driver. Hat off; have passed three churches.

j 14. K. Krohn 11446 Juuka. — To Lapland. Lapp's three sons. First, as bullet; second, as gray hen. Hat falls. Lies 5 km back. Paid with black cow. Man had forgotten to say prayer when closing window and Lapp makes cow go through window. Hence the saying when some one threatens at nothing: Is he going to take cow from hindmost stall?

j 14. K. Krohn 12571 Kaavi. — Räsänen from Kortteinen village is troubled by evil spirit. He goes to Lapland and is rid of it. Kekri eve. Says he would like to be home in the morning. "If you will promise the hindmost black cow."

k (South Österbotten).

k 1. S. Korpela 39 Teuva. — Man in sedge meadow. Whirlwind carries off hay. Man throws knife and goes to look for knife. Goes to sea in a boat which carries him to island where there is a Lapp's cabin. When he is asked to eat he sees his knife. Lapp reprimands him for throwing it into his thigh. Before he goes man must promise black cow from doorpost. Lapp tells him to tie cow to post in yard on three consecutive Thursdays. Both sit on pole and are seen at man's home. First Thursday, ox tied to post. Whirlwind lifts and drops it. Second Thursday, cow tied to post, is likewise lifted and dropped. Third Thursday, ox tied to post but cow is carried off.

k 2. S. Korpela 38 Teuva. — Whirlwind scatters hay of man in sedge-meadow. Man swears, spits, and throws knife. Falls sick and goes to Lapp wisemen for cure. Asked to eat; sees own knife on table in leg of reindeer. Had thrown it into Lapp's thigh. Holiday eve. Lonesome. Lapp will take him home in time for holiday bath for black cow at doorpost. Three sons. First, speed of gray hen; second, bullet; third, thought. Man placed in rear of trough is home at once. Tells wife to substitute poorer cow. Cow gone; bellowing audible.

k 3. Korpi 11 Ylihärmä or Isokyrö. — Whirlwind blows toward farmer working out of doors. Out of fear farmer throws knife and feels sharp pain in thigh. To Lapland for cure. Sees knife on table. Master says he had been hit in thigh with knife. Cured. Wants to go home. Lapp demands best cow. Speed of bullet chosen, since gray hen is not swift enough. Man gets in sleigh; Lapp is driver. Told to get out on second bump. Farmer pretends to forget promise; Lapp reminds him and cow is brought out. Bellowing heard as it disappears.

k 4. J. Kotkanen 10 Laihia. — Farmer spends many years in Lapland. Holiday eve and desires to be at home. Lapp will take him for cow nearest door. Lapp takes him in whirlwind. Tells servants to move cow to another stall, but the cow is gone.

k 5. M. N. Möykky 6 Isojoki. — Man throws knife at whirlwind. Becomes troubled. Goes north to search for knife. On holiday eve arrives in Lapland. At meal sees own knife. Reprimanded for throwing it into master's thigh. Man wishes to be home for holiday dinner. Lapp will take him for large black ox nearest door. Speed of bullet not fast enough; they decide to go a hundred times faster. Sit on branch of spruce. Cap falls off, but it lies three churches back. At home man tells servant girl to substitute small ox, but the large ox is gone.

k 6. K. Krohn 15638 Himanka. — Poor fields cause man of Lohtaja parish to go to Lapland. On way thither throws knife at passing torch. At farm he is given food and sees own knife on table. Mistress reprimands him for throwing knife at husband who is now ill in bed with wound in his thigh.

k 7. K. Krohn 15639 Himanka. — Man goes to Lapland for knowledge. Christmas eve. Wishes to be home to know what they have for dinner. Lapp bets he will bring sample of everything while man is in bathhouse; the stake to be the black ox; and as additional proof the man's wife's stocking. At home wife, who knows nothing of Lapp, searches for stocking. Man comes home and brings back stocking. She is surprised that he has it since she had it after he had left.

l (Middle Österbotten).

l 1. E. Keränen 107 Kärsämäki. — Kekri eve a Finn in Lapland for his health wishes to be home. Lapp will take him for black spotted cow at door. Tells man to lie on bench, to move nearer middle at the first motion, near end the next time, and to drop off third time. Man obeys and awakes at head of own table. Spotted cow gone.

I 2. E. Keränen 117 Kärsämäki. — Lapp travels in whirlwind over harvestfield. Man strikes it with knife because it scatters straw. Knife disappears; man becomes ill. Goes to see Lapp wisemen. Sees knife in cabinwall. Tells Lapp how it had been lost. Lapp asks why he did not throw piece of bread. Journey to Lapland alone brought him cure.

I 3. K. Krohn 860 Piippola. — Cows from hindmost stall disappear.

I 4. K. Krohn 1979 Pyhäjärvi. — Man at Haapamäki stays long in Lapland. Christmas eve. Wishes to be home. Three brothers and father want bull for trip. Youngest, like gray hen; second, black cock; eldest, like thought. They put him to sleep at head of table with his axe for pillow. In morning awakes at home. Bull gone.

I 5. K. Krohn 2332 Pyhäjärvi. — Man in Lapland wishes quick return. Lapp will take him before morning for black cow at door. Between thought and bullet chooses bullet. In morning is sleeping at home at head of table. Goes to cow-stable; cow gone.

I 6. K. Krohn 2336 Pyhäjärvi. — Farmer's wife, an excellent butter-maker, gets 50 kg. of butter from a single cow in summer and 30 kg. in winter. They have seven cows. The young wife suspects her old husband of unfaithfulness and neglects cattle, which yield only 10 kg. of butter a year. Husband reproves her and she flames up in anger. He regrets his action and falls sick. Dreams advise him to go to Lappish wizards for cure. He goes. Gives a bottle of wine to a sage who sees the cause of the farmer's trouble and cures it. Christmas eve. Sage will take him for the black bull at the doorpost. Tells the farmer to go to sleep on the sofa. Farmer awakens in his own room. Bull gone.

I 7. K. Krohn 2487 Pyhäjärvi. — Christmas eve. Three brothers. Like bird; like bullet; like thought. Third chosen. Black bull.

l 8. K. Krohn 2672 Pyhäjärvi. — Man in Lapland comes home for Kekri. Black spotted cow. Three brothers. When he falls on boards of bath-house, he must turn on the other side or he will be carried back. First brother, like black cock; second, bullet; third, thought.

l 9. K. Krohn 2876 Haapajärvi. — To Lapland. Black bull.

l 10. K. Krohn 3061 Nivala. — Sick person went to old man and woman in Lapland. The Lapps sat on millstone in boiling torrent, woman above, man below, between them a pot containing the money of three kings. They conjured, and received cow from the person whom they cured. The cow returned in a single night.

l 11. K. Krohn 3062 Nivala. — Christmas eve. Farmer Jaakola from church village. Black spotted bull. Three brothers.

l 12. K. S. Paulaharju 432 Muhos. — Man visits Lapp wiseman who alone could cure him. Man wishes to be home. Lapp will take him for bull in stall nearest door, Lapp asks if he wants to go like bullet or gray hen. Latter chosen. Hears as in dream lowing of bull. Roads meet there. Awakes in morning at home. Bull gone.

m (East Österbotten).

m 1. K. Krohn 0130 Sotkamo. — Told of Korhonen family at Sipola's farm in Vihtamäki village at Sotkamo three hundred years ago. — A man who has not learned to to read inspite of his parents' scolding that there is one God,[1] goes to Lapland to learn witchcraft. Meets a woman at whom he had thrown an ax the previous summer, when she was traveling in a whirlwind. Man visits home of most famous sage. Sage goes to man's home in an magic

---

[1] The incoherence is due to the narrator.

arrow and brings back the wife's ring.[1] Kekri eve. Lapp will take him for the black cow at the doorpost. The man's cap flies off; it lies nine churches behind. Awakes Kekri morning at his own table. Women go to cowhouse, but the cow is gone. The man comforts his wife.

m 2. K. Krohn 0667 Sotkamo. — Old farmer of Sipola at Vihtamäki village buries money and lays charms he cannot break on it. Goes to sages in Lapland for advice. Sage tells him to fell tree across a river and lay copper wire along it. By walking on the wire he will comply with the requirement of walking on copper bridge. On Kekri eve he wishes to be home. Lapp will take him for black cow in the hindmost stall. Lapp covers man with wife's shirt. Man falls asleep. Awakes in morning at Sotkamo and tells servants to look in stable. Cow is gone. Sipola's net caught the most fish because he had worn the shirt of the Lapp's wife.

m 3. K. Krohn 16466 Sotkamo. — Kekri eve a man in Lapland wishes to go home. Lapp will take him for black cow in hindmost stall. Man is incredulous. Lapp volunteers to bring ring off man's wife. Wife's finger itches; she takes off ring and lays it on table. Lapp carries it to man. They start home. Man's hat catches on church steeple, but it lies now five churches behind and is not recovered. Arrive at midnight. In morning he tells women to look for black cow, but it is gone. Man says it had paid for his ride.

m 4. K. Krohn 0169 Ristijärvi. — On Kekri Perttu of Pyhäntä village wishes to return home from Lapland. Lapp will take him for what stands in the hindmost stall in stable. Coming home, he bumps his foot on cross of church. Asks Lapp what it was. Lapp says it is too far back to speak about it. In morning, when he arrives, he

---

[1] Cf. j 6.

goes to stable. An ox of three summers which stood in last stall is gone, but the head is left. The skull is in Eskola's attic today.

m 5. K. Krohn 0261 b Ristijärvi. — Man of Eskola seeks advice in Lapland to aid him in locating his farm luckily. Lapp tells him to choose a spot in a valley so that water runs in from all sides and out from one. Kekri; he wishes to be home. Lapp's three sons: like bird, like fish, "as one thinks, or if you don't think, by jumping". Lapp wants ox and leaves its head.

m 6. K. Krohn 604 a Sotkamo. — Man from Pyhäntä village who was in Lapland returned on Kekri.

s (Ingria).

s 1. Uudenkirkon Kansanopisto 2 Tuuteri. — Man from Hirvonen village goes to Lapp sorcerers because grasshoppers chirp in his ears. Is cured. Wishes to return Christmas eve. Lapp offers speed of bird, of bullet, and "as here and there". Lapp will take him for black heifer, but the man has been gone so long that he is unaware of its existence. He accepts. Lapp puts him in tub and tells him not to fetch hat if it falls. Lapp makes a sign. In one swoop man is at home. Goes to stable. Heifer is gone.

E (Estonia).

E 1. M. I. Eisen p. 36810 Kadrina by Rakvere (Wesenberg). — Wizards carry everything to Lapland. They carry a man in a whirlwind. He appears at a house there and is commanded to remain as a servant. He obeys and works like a bear for food alone. After seven years he longs for wife and children. Lapp will take him for spotted ox. Lapp puts him in a vehicle shaped like a pig's toe. Man crosses the sea to his own country and arrives Christmas eve. In the meantime his wife had married again and has had two children. Great surprise at his return. Man goes to cow-stable. Spotted ox is gone.

E 2. J. Hurt III, 9, p. 385 Kodavere by Tartu (Dorpat). — Farmers carry brandy. Man meets wolf with goose in its mouth and strikes wolf so that the goose falls. Man throws goose in wagon. Horse grows tired and falls behind the others. Man sees fire in woods. Old man says, "Now the wolves will eat you". — Man promises ox and throws goose on ground. Arrives home. Wife locks ox in barn, but it is gone in the morning. Man comforts wife.[1]

E 3. J. Hurt I, 4, p. 731. Kanepi by Võru (Werro). — Farmers carry brandy. Man meets wolf with goose in its mouth and takes the goose. Man throws goose in wagon. Horse grows tired and falls behind the others. Man sees fire in woods and a crowd of wolves. The leader in the middle threatens that he will be eaten up. Man promises ox which he believes is standing behind a locked door tied with three chains. During the man's absence the ox breaks loose. Man comforts wife.[2]

FS (Swedes in Finland).

FS. Sv. litt. sällsk. 102 p. 9. Vestenfjärd south of Turku (Åbo). — Finnish sailor is in Stockholm Christmas eve. Lapp will take him home for red and white cow. Lapp's three daughters offer speeds: eldest, as bird flies; second, as bullet; youngest, as thought. Sailor accepts third and is at home. Cow disappears.

N (Norway).

N 1. P. M. Søegard, *I Fjeldbygerne*, p. 107 (Valdres). A farmer goes out to shoot a bear. Some one calls from

[1] This may not belong to the cycle of the Black Ox. —
[2] This, like E 2, may not belong to the cycle of the Black Ox.

the mountain, "Look out for your pig, neighbor". Neighbor answers, "He can't kill it because he has not washed today". The farmer has water with him and washes, then kills the bear, skins it, and lays his knife on a birch stump. He wraps the meat in the skin. He finds the knife is gone. He is in town Christmas eve to sell butter. Wood spirit in the form of an old man passes him with the lost knife in a sheath. The farmer wants to go home. The old man invites him to ride on sleigh runners. The farmer asks where he found the knife. The old man says, "On a stump". He wants the farmer's large gray pig, not for the ride but in return for his "pig", i.e., the bear. He tells the man not to look behind. The man does so and sees the spirit's home in the open mountain. The man's head becomes crooked. The gray pig disappears, but the farmer has good luck with pigs thereafter.

S (Sweden).

S 1. Hylten Cavallius, *Wärend och Wirdarne,* II p. LIV. Man throws a knife at a whirlwind and strikes a witch in the thigh. Later he is lost in the woods and arrives at a Lapp's cabin where a Lapp woman gives him food and asks him if the knife is familiar. He cannot find his way home. She puts him into a sappho (Lappish sleigh), and puts a rope with three knots before him. When he opens one knot, he goes through the air; when he opens the second, he goes faster; when he opens the third, he goes so fast that, on the stopping of the sleigh, he is thrown to the ground and breaks his leg.

S 2. J. V. Palmqvist, *Rester av primitiv religion bland Wärmlands Finnbefolkning,* p. 175. Man from Norra By goes to Lapland for aid from wise men against a wicked neighbor who has set a bear on his cattle. Christmas is near and he wishes to be home. The Lapp promises to take him home for a cow and a copper kettle. The man assents. The Lapp seats him on a stump fastened with a rope having three knots. By letting out the knots one by one he travels faster and faster. At home he sends back stump, cow, and kettle. He arrives for Christmas porridge. In the spring a big bear appears in his neighbor's cattle yard; it can only be killed with a silver bullet.

www.ingramcontent.com/pod-product-compliance
Lightning Source LLC
Chambersburg PA
CBHW071156090426
42736CB00012B/2353